TOMORROW'S CHURCH

Catholic · Evangelical · Reformed

By the Author:

SAINTS ON MAIN STREET

STRANGERS NO LONGER

PETER DAY

TOMORROW'S CHURCH

Catholic · Evangelical · Reformed

102318

THE SEABURY PRESS · NEW YORK

Copyright © 1969 by The Seabury Press, Incorporated
Library of Congress Catalog Card Number: 68-24009
Design by Stefan Salter
620-1268-C-5
Printed in the United States of America

An Original Seabury Paperback

Contents

I.	"All in Each Place"	7
II.	"Unity . . . God's Will and His Gift"	16
III.	"The One Apostolic Faith"	27
IV.	"Joining in Common Prayer"	41
V.	"Baptized into Jesus Christ"	52
VI.	"Breaking the One Bread"	61
VII.	"Ministry . . . Accepted by All"	70
VIII.	The Ministry of the Members	82
IX.	"The Tasks to Which God Calls His People"	89
X.	"Brought by the Holy Spirit . . ."	99
XI.	"All Places and All Ages"	111

APPENDIX: Some Recent Statements on Faith, Order, and Unity — 123

1. African Methodist Episcopal Church — 125
2. The Disciples of Christ — 130
3. The Episcopal Church — 133
4. The Presbyterian Church in the United States — 145
5. The United Church of Christ — 152
6. The United Methodist Church — 159

7. The United Presbyterian Church   167
8. Discussion Between Roman Catholics
   and Anglicans   182
9. Discussion Between Roman Catholic
   and Reformed Theologians   185

I

"All in Each Place"

Church unity is in the air these days. In Europe, Asia, Africa, Australia, South America, and North America, groups of Christians are coming together to talk about their common commitment to Jesus Christ and their joint responsibility to be obedient to his will in and for the world.

Some of these groups are made up of officially appointed church leaders and theologians wrestling with the issues of doctrine, worship, ministry, and sacraments which must be settled before divided churches can unite. Others are local study groups sponsored by a congregation or a group of congregations. They too may be concerned with theological formulations, but they also have to think about what needs to be done in their community right now to bring the redemptive power of the gospel to bear on people's lives. For the local church is above all the place where Christian faith must be lived out in its fullness, in both words and deeds.

The level of Christian dialogue that is entitled to be called the official level varies from one church to another. Indeed, this is one of the persistent difficulties of relationships between churches. Nobody can make a final decision about Roman

Catholic doctrine except a Pope or an international council of bishops. Nobody can tell an Episcopalian or a Presbyterian what to believe except his national governing body—General Convention or General Assembly. Among such churches any international body is purely advisory in character. For Baptists, the final power of decision is in the local congregation. National conventions of Baptists—or international ones—have no authority to commit the local church.

There are both theological and historical reasons for these varieties of church structure. If we are really serious about church unity, however, we must recognize that every level of church government and life is an important level. Nationally organized churches must be concerned about their international fellowship of faith. They must also be concerned that regional groups (dioceses, presbyteries, etc.) and local congregations understand and agree with the positions taken by their representatives in unity discussions; otherwise they would face the possibility of dividing their own church while uniting with another.

The Protestant, Anglican, and Eastern Orthodox churches have been engaged in dialogue and various forms of practical cooperation for a long while—about sixty years, in fact. The ongoing movement which has brought this about is known as the ecumenical movement. The word "ecumenical" means "worldwide" or "universal," and in church usage it is applied to the great church councils of the early centuries which settled important controversies about the doctrine of the Trinity and the person of Christ.

Organized ecumenical activity is headed up internationally in the World Council of Churches, and in the United States in the National Council of Churches, which offer their member churches means of speaking and acting together on many matters of Christian concern as well as opportunities for study and discussion on questions of faith and order. These bodies have, of course, no authority over the churches that belong to them, and therefore are not in a position to discuss unions between particular churches. They have done much, however, to build a common "universe of discourse" among Christians, arriving at agreed statements on such issues as the Scriptures, the sacraments, and the ministry, which have helped to clear away long-standing disagreements.

The great new ecumenical fact of the present decade is the entry of the Roman Catholic Church into the ecumenical scene, as the result of the amazing leadership of Pope John XXIII and the Second Vatican Council. Seeing what John accomplished in four short years of (as he said) opening a window and letting fresh air blow through the Church, helps us to understand how Jesus could accomplish all that he did in a ministry of only three years.

Until the Roman Catholic Church became a part of the ecumenical picture, the ecumenical movement could not be truly ecumenical. It could not help appearing to be an effort to organize half the Christians of the world against the other half. Now, however, the Vatican Secretariat for Christian Unity is engaged in active dialogue with the World Council of Churches; with the worldwide Anglican Communion (represented in America by the Episcopal Church); with the Lutheran World Federation; with the Methodists; and with a steadily increasing list of other churches.

In the U.S.A., similarly, the Roman Catholic Church has set up the Bishops' Committee for Ecumenical and Interreligious Affairs, which is holding consultations on a comparable scale with Eastern Orthodox, Episcopal, Lutheran, Reformed, Methodist, Disciples, and other churches, as well as with the National Council of Churches.

Two excellent study books have been developed by the Roman Catholic Church and the National Council of Churches working together—*Living Room Dialogues,* and *Second Liv-*

*ing Room Dialogues.** They are being widely used by local interchurch discussion groups.

The annual Week of Prayer for Christian Unity, presently sponsored by Roman Catholics and the National Council of Churches together, with common posters and service leaflets, is observed more widely every year. For 1968, local churches ordered 1,500,000 leaflets. The pattern of theological education is steadily becoming more ecumenical, as seminaries make use of each other's facilities and personnel, including Roman Catholic seminaries and colleges. Many other common projects and activities are being undertaken; and it would be impossible to keep track of all the varied honors and courtesies and friendly contacts that are being exchanged day by day.

Certainly, the goal of Christian unity is the unity of all Christians, not just some of them. For example, the Episcopal Church in its 1967 General Convention affirmed that "the object of this Church's ecumenical policy is to press toward the visible unity of the whole Christian Fellowship in the faith and truth of Jesus Christ, developing and sharing in its various dialogues and consultations in such a way that the goal be neither obscured nor compromised and that each separate activity be a step toward the fulness of unity for which our Saviour prayed."

When one considers the many different varieties of Christians today, and the barriers of doctrine, worship, ministry, and custom that divide them, this goal seems very far away and difficult to achieve. But every big problem can be divided into smaller and more manageable parts. And many parts of the problem of unity are being solved one by one.

* William B. Greenspun, C.S.P., and William A. Norgren, co-editors, *Living Room Dialogues* (New York: Department of Publication Services, National Council of Churches, and Glen Rock, N.J.: Paulist Press, 1965). William B. Greenspun, C.S.P., and Cynthia C. Wedel, co-editors. *Second Living Room Dialogues* (New York: Friendship Press, and Glen Rock, N.J.: Paulist Press, 1967).

Where denominations in this country have shared a common theological tradition, they have made great progress. The Methodists, for example, were once three major denominations, but now are one, and that one united with the Evangelical United Brethren Church in 1968. Six Lutheran churches have become two—the Lutheran Church in America and the American Lutheran Church; and these two have entered into close cooperation with the Lutheran Church–Missouri Synod and the synod of evangelical Lutheran Churches in the Lutheran Council in the U.S.A. Three Presbyterian denominations have come together in the United Presbyterian Church in the U.S.A. The Presbyterian Church in the U.S. (Southern Presbyterian) did not join in this union, but is currently considering unity with the Reformed Church in America.

Even more significant, in terms of overcoming major differences in forms of church government, was the union of the Congregational-Christian Church with the Evangelical and Reformed Church to form the United Church of Christ, combining congregational and presbyterial polity.

The boldest and most far-reaching effort toward union currently under consideration in the United States is the Consultation on Church Union. It includes nine churches of varied background who are working together to devise a plan of union which will be truly Catholic, truly evangelical, and truly reformed.

In alphabetical order, the nine are: the African Methodist Episcopal Church; the African Methodist Episcopal Zion Church; the Christian Churches (Disciples of Christ); the Christian Methodist Episcopal Church; the Episcopal Church; the Presbyterian Church in the U.S.; the United Church of Christ; the United Methodist Church; the United Presbyterian Church in the U.S.A.

Observers from many other churches participate in the Consultation's deliberations—Roman Catholic, Eastern Orthodox, Baptist, and Lutheran, to name a few. For it is the Consultation's intention not just to work out a compromise among the nine churches represented, but to be a part of the mainstream of Christian life and thought. If and when they do all come together, they will be a very numerous fellowship indeed—some 25 million strong, of many races (with a higher proportion of Negroes than the general population), and with diverse gifts and talents to bring to the common life.

Union discussions of comparable scope are going on in many other parts of the world—discussions with a spectrum of participation ranging from Anglicanism to Congregationalism. In some, the participants include Baptists, and in one they include Quakers. Recently, under the auspices of the World Council of Churches, a Consultation on Church Union Negotiations was held in which about fifty participants from twenty-three nations compared notes.*

So far, only one united church has actually come into being with such a wide range of church traditions—the Church of South India, including Anglicans, Methodists, Presbyterians, and Congregationalists. Both the experience of this church and the work being done in other parts of the world are important resources for the thinking and dialogue in America.

The American Consultation on Church Union has gone further than some of those in other nations, but not as far as some others. Its major product up to now is a document entitled *Principles of Church Union,* adopted in 1966 and transmitted to the membership of the nine participating churches for study and report as each church arranges. The text of this important document, incorporated in a small book entitled *Consultation on Church Union, 1967,* can be obtained from local bookstores or from Forward Movement Publica-

* The report of the Consultation appears in *Midstream,* quarterly journal of the Council on Christian Unity of the Disciples of Christ, Vol. VI, No. 3 (Spring, 1968).

tions, 412 Sycamore Street, Cincinnati, Ohio, 45202, at 25 cents a copy.

It sets forth what the representatives of a very large group of American Christians find themselves able to say together about the faith of the Church, the worship of the Church, the sacraments of the Church, and the ministry of the Church.

Do these statements represent the thinking not only of the people who framed them but of the rank and file of their churches? Do they provide a basis for going forward with the difficult task of shaping the structure of a united Church? This is a question which can be answered only by the members of the nine churches themselves as they read and discuss the Consultation's report.

Indeed, the men and women who framed *Principles of Church Union* realize that it is not yet a complete and final basis for unity. The representatives of one church in their official report to its governing body put the matter frankly in these words:

As the Consultation continues its work, it will be essential that its members be guided and supported by the informed judgment of the churches they represent. The Commission is therefore asking this General Convention to provide for thorough and systematic study in every diocese. . . .

Such study will make plain the notable and unexpected degree of common affirmation even now possible to the delegates of the churches in the Consultation. The ten churches represent a broad spectrum of Christian traditions unprecedented in modern ecumenical discussion. To some, the recitation of a creed is customary practice; to others, creeds are almost unknown. In one church, formal liturgical worship is the norm; in another, it hardly exists. Infant Baptism represents no problem to some, while it seems utterly anomalous to others. Bishops are seen in widely different lights in different churches. Priesthood is a commonplace word on some lips and, on others, a word to be said with the greatest gentleness to describe him who is the universal priest. So it goes, in every sensitive area of the Church's life.

Against this background, it is remarkable that the Consultation was able to make the unitive and fundamental affirmations to be found in *Principles*. [The report then quotes passages on the Holy Communion, the Creeds, the ministry, baptism, and worship, and continues:]

The Commission's support of the Consultation, and the recommendations with regard to it, therefore, arise not from any exaggerated claims as to what Principles of Church Union represents, but rather from deep gratitude for what the dialogue has already accomplished and an equally deep confidence in the process of the dialogue itself. The Commission believes that the agreements so far reached should be commended as a significant advance toward Christian unity, that they should be given systematic and responsible study, and that this Church's participation in the Consultation should continue, looking toward the development, when such development is possible, of a plan of union that could then be brought to the constituent churches for their consideration. To ask more than this would be to go beyond the point the Consultation itself has reached. To ask less than this would be, the Commission believes, faithless to what God has already led the Consultation to find.*

Thus, *Principles of Church Union* must be regarded as work in progress—work in which every member of the participating churches is asked to join. Among the laity of these churches—and among the clergy as well—are some who feel that the differences between the churches are unimportant and that some simple compromise can easily be worked out. They need to find how deep and difficult the problems are. And there are others who feel that the differences are so great that union is an idle dream. They need to find out what great progress has already been made, and to sense the power of the one Spirit working within each of the divided churches to bring them into the unity which is Christ's will for his Church. As

* Report of the Joint Commission on Ecumenical Relations to the 1967 General Convention of the Episcopal Church, pp. 9:16-20.

Jesus said, in another connection: "With men, it is impossible, but with God all things are possible."

To view the problem in these terms means that the nine churches involved in the Consultation cannot look upon their coming together as the final goal. As *Principles of Church Union* says (Preamble, paragraph f): "It must be a uniting as well as a united Church. This means emphasizing the united Church's incomplete and provisional character, its own desire to press steadily forward toward wider unity, both national and international. The separate churches desire not merely to form a new and larger denomination, but to embark on a pilgrimage whose only ultimate goal can be the unity of the whole Body."

Accordingly, dialogues with the Roman Catholics, with the Eastern Orthodox, with Lutherans, Baptists, Pentecostals, Conservative Evangelicals—with any who bear the name of Christ—cannot be regarded as a set of mutually opposed or competitive activities but, rather, as a necessity if the Consultation on Church Union is to attain its goal. This applies not only to its ultimate goal, but to its immediate one of joining the nine churches, for their union should consciously aim at drawing closer to a divine—and human—pattern in which all Christians have a place.

> *Grant to your Church, merciful God, that, being gathered together in unity by the Holy Spirit, it may manifest your power among all peoples, to the glory of your name; through Jesus Christ our Lord, who lives and reigns with you and the same Spirit, one God, for endless ages. Amen.*

II

"Unity...God's Will and His Gift"

A two-day laymen's conference on church unity was near its end. Previously the speakers had discussed the work of the great cooperative agencies of the churches, the World and National Councils, and the union discussions going on between churches. They had talked about the biblical imperatives of unity, the need of mankind for a united witness to the gospel of Jesus Christ, the need to eliminate duplication of effort, all the theological, practical, and moral reasons why Christians should unite.

Finally, one man spoke up in honest bewilderment. "I have just one question," he said. "Why? Why? I just can't see any reason why the churches should do anything different from what they are doing now."

Perhaps this man was thinking of the subject in much the same terms as if it were a proposal to unite the Rotary, Kiwanis, and Lion's clubs, with the ultimate aim of one big service club replacing all the others. On its institutional side the Church does have some of the aspects of a service club, plus a service station, and there doesn't seem to be any compelling reason why all service clubs and service stations should be under one management. There is a strong individualistic strain in American Christianity which views religion as a private relationship between oneself and Christ, and a particular church as only one of a number of possible resources for establishing and maintaining this relationship.

This strong personal piety is one of the good things about American Christianity. But it must become a part of a more-full-bodied understanding of our relationship to Christ and to each other in Christ. Among the biblical phrases describing the Church, one of the favorites of the Second Vatican Council was "the people of God." As I Peter 2:9 puts it, "You are a chosen race, a royal priesthood, a holy nation, God's own people, that you may declare the wonderful deeds of him who called you out of darkness into his marvelous light."

The Christian, accordingly, is a part of a vast fellowship in time and space, the fellowship of those who have Jesus Christ in common. This fellowship is the Church, and barriers of division have no place within it.

In *Second Living Room Dialogues,* Dr. Theodore O. Wedel quotes a minister of a prosperous suburban church as saying: "This is no longer a Christian fellowship. These are members of a Christian church who pay, and pay mighty well, to be serviced spiritually. In a way, I am not much better off, in some ways worse off, than the gas station attendant. They pay him to keep their cars in running condition. They pay me somehow to do something that will keep their lives from blowing into bits."

Dr. Wedel goes on:

Pietistic individualism, on either Roman Catholic or Protestant soil, did not reveal its weakness in days when the average Christian was still surrounded by a community life in village or town nourished by the charity of the Gospel. The powers of the Holy Spirit performed their healing and strengthening tasks in the Christian family and in the closely knit Christian community throughout the week, and were not dependent for finding avenues of expression solely upon a formalized worship on Sunday. . . .

Our problem is the reverse of that confronting our forefathers. For us the problem consists of recreating, within and alongside the church's institutional activities, the Christian community in which Christian charity can bring to men and women the gift of the glorous liberty of the children of God. For if we turn for a vision of what Christian fellowship might be when true to the norm of the New Testament, the wonder and glory of the fellowship of the Holy Spirit leaps to life. Here, where "there is neither Jew nor Greek, there is neither slave nor free, there is neither male nor female; for you are all one in Christ Jesus" (Galatians 3:28)— exclusion is apostasy. Here is a brotherhood of penitence and gratitude. . . . Here is a "colony of heaven" in the midst of a dying world, one that enjoys a foretaste of a new heaven and earth beyond mortality's dread end.*

Yet, the Christian congregation in a united Church will not externally be very different from the unecumenical Christian congregation of the past. It can be spiritually lively, or feeble, or dead, and it will have the same round of worship, Christian education, and activities of various kinds. Entering into union with millions of fellow Christians should greatly strengthen and deepen the parish's understanding of itself as a company of the people of God, but its task will basically be the same that it always was: to build up the discipleship which brings us to the truth that makes us free.

In its deepest sense, the task of the ecumenical movement is not to unite churches, but to unite mankind in the body of Christ. Again and again, whether at high levels or low in this movement, we shall find that the unity of the Church and the holiness, the God centeredness, of the Church are inextricably intertwined; and that these two are also deeply entwined with

* Theodore O. Wedel, *The Gospel in a Strange New World* (Philadelphia: Westminster Press, 1963). Copyright © 1963, W. L. Jenkins. Used by permission. Quoted in *Second Living Room Dialogues*, pp. 254 ff.

the other two notes of the Church—catholicity and apostolicity.

Thus, for the layman to be a better Christian within the context of his own church's tradition—more deeply devoted to God, more active in his participation in the Church's worship, more courageous and determined in living in the world as one of the fellowship whom Christ has made his own—is without question the most important ecumenical work a layman can do.

It is far more important—and, in the deepest sense, more ecumenical—to give a cup of cold water to one of Christ's little ones than to read a book about Methodism or visit the local Presbyterian church. It is more ecumenical, because it has a more powerful bearing on the question of making mankind one in Christ.

Because of this world-embracing goal, the parish of today finds many urgent items on its agenda which were not prominent there a generation ago: civil rights; the war on poverty; questions of national and international morality. Church people find themselves involved with non-Christians and even with nonbelievers in projects to bring men in *this* life and *this* world some of the good things which we believe God means them to have. The ecumenical movement broadens out into "secular ecumenism," in response to Christ's emphatic statement: "Whoever does the will of my Father in heaven is my brother, and sister, and mother" (Matthew 12:50).

Nevertheless, the task of uniting churches is, on equally solid scriptural grounds, an important part of the ecumenical movement. In the New Testament, as in modern usage, the word "church" can refer either to a local Christian congregation or to the whole body of believers in Christ. But another modern meaning of the word "church" as it appears in "the Episcopal Church," "the Methodist Church," "the Roman Catholic Church," etc.—the denominational meaning—is contrary to both the letter and the spirit of the Bible.

St. Paul describes the Christians of his time as *one body*—the body of Christ, of which all Christ's people are members. Jesus, in the Gospel according to St. John, both prophesies and prays for the unity of his flock.

In John 10:14 ff., he says: "I am the good shepherd; I know my own and my own know me, as the Father knows me and I know the Father; and I lay down my life for the sheep. And I have other sheep, that are not of this fold; I must bring them also, and they will heed my voice. *So there shall be one flock, one shepherd*" (italics added).

And in the seventeenth chapter, which is the great charter of the ecumenical movement, he prays: "I do not pray for these only, but also for those who are to believe in me through their word, that they may all be one; even as thou, Father, art in me, and I in thee, that they also may be in us, so that the world may believe that thou hast sent me. The glory which thou hast given me I have given to them, that they may be one even as we are one, . . ."

In these passages the unity of the Christian fellowship is seen as a reflection and manifestation to the world of the glory of God, and as a sharing in the relationship of Christ with his heavenly Father.

So in the Apostles' Creed, we confess our belief in "The holy Catholic Church," not in a particular segment of it; and in the Nicene Creed, even more emphatically, we speak of *"one holy Catholic and Apostolic Church"* (italics added).

A Church divided into denominations obscures the nature of the Church as set forth in the Scriptures and the Creeds.

We have become so accustomed to denominationalism that we take it for granted that different denominations are unrelated entities, and that uniting them is an effort to put together oil and water or fish and fowl. But this is an illusion, an upside-down view of the truth about the Church. It is like those pictures in children's books of an upside-down stairway that turns itself right-side up while you are looking at it. The Church, the collection of visible, earthly, existential churches with their buildings and ministers and lay boards and parishioners, *is* one right now. As the Book of Common Prayer says, "The Church is the Body of which Jesus Christ is the Head, and all baptized people are the members." Roman Catholics, Eastern Orthodox, Methodists, Lutherans, Presbyterians, Episcopalians, Baptists, and many others are members of that body and share in a single spiritual identity. Their task is to clear up the fearful mess that they have made of their relationships within the one Church.

After all, when St. Paul told the Corinthians that they were the body of Christ (I Corinthians 12:12 ff.) he was not paying them a compliment. Quite the opposite—he was criticizing them for their factionalism. He was urging them to live out in action the common life they already possessed. This life was theirs—and is ours—as God's gift to his Church through Jesus Christ.

Sometimes a distinction is made between "Christian unity" and "Church union"—often by people who favor the former but not the latter. Christian unity is seen as a matter of the spirit, while Church union is thought of in terms of structures and rules and administration of programs. Those who are working to bring the churches together, however, insist that if Christian unity is genuine it must express itself in Church union.

There is truth on both sides of the case. The New Testament does not present the picture of a highly structured "super-church" with official mission boards and publishing houses and regular sessions of national, diocesan, and parochial governing bodies. What is said about the oneness of Christ's followers refers primarily to loving and supportive relationships between Christian persons. But it is plain even in the primitive church of the New Testament that people who live a common life do need organs to express that life. Decisions had to be made, abuses had to be dealt with, common enterprises had to be brought to a successful conclusion. Man is an incurably social being. He cannot live out his life in one-to-one relationships, and wherever two or three people are gathered together the process of voting begins—even when they are gathered in the name of Christ.

Church union represents a genuine giving of self to the cause of unity. The Prayer Book prayer For the Unity of God's People speaks of being "united in one holy bond of truth and peace, of faith and charity," and it is true that the bond of charity—of love, whether earthly or heavenly—involves a commitment to sacrifice one's own desires for the sake of others. Chaucer, in one of the *Canterbury Tales,* speaks of the "faire chain of love" given to man by God. We are never more complete persons than when we accept binding relationships with our brothers.

But, if it is agreed that true Christian unity involves arriving at decisions, coping with abuses, and carrying out common enterprises, we face the first, and possibly the most basic, problem of Church unity. It may be expressed in four words: "Who's in charge here?"

The answer is easier for those who have only dipped their fingertips in ecumenical thinking and dialogue than for those who have been immersed in it for a long time.

The easy early answers usually work out to a projection of the basic forms of one's own church life on a grand scale, whether episcopal, presbyterial, or congregational, leavened with a promise that there will be much room for diversity. But then we find that what seems simply and obviously right to us is by no means so obviously right to others.

Perhaps the most that can be said about the nature of church unity is the statement of the Third Assembly of the

World Council of Churches at New Delhi, India, in 1961:

We believe that the unity which is both God's will and his gift to his Church is being made visible as all in each place who are baptized into Jesus Christ and confess him as Lord and Saviour are brought by the Holy Spirit into one fully committed fellowship, holding the one apostolic faith, preaching the one gospel, breaking the one bread, joining in common prayer, and having a corporate life reaching out in witness and service to all and who at the same time are united with the whole Christian fellowship in all places and all ages in such wise that ministry and members are accepted by all, and that all can act and speak together as occasion requires for the tasks to which God calls his people.

It is for such unity that we believe we must pray and work.

This pregnant paragraph sounds the basic themes of the life of a united Church—baptism, confession of faith in Christ, the fellowship of the Holy Spirit, holding and preaching the apostolic doctrine, common prayer and Holy Communion, a common life of witness and service to the world—all at the local level, for unity is first and foremost a local thing. But to be complete, the local Christian fellowship must be a part of the whole people of God in all places and throughout history; membership and ministry must be acceptable to the whole of that vast Christian continuum in space and time; and the Church throughout the world must have means of speaking with one voice and acting with one purpose from time to time as obedience to God may require.

Indeed, as the chapter headings show, this book is essentially a report of the way in which American Christians are working together to make the New Delhi statement come true in their life together.

The particular forms of ministry and government which may fit its prescription, the basic doctrines and sacramental practices, the nature of the tasks of witness and service to which the Church is called both locally and in wider settings

—these are the problems to which the Christians of today must find answers if they are to be true to the New Testament conception of the Church.

It would not be too difficult a task, perhaps, if the churches did not have so much history behind them. The ancient ministry of bishops, priests, and deacons might be an entirely satisfactory solution of the problem of the ministry, if Protestant Christians did not have such vivid memories of the abuses in the hierarchy which triggered the Reformation. So too with other forms of ministry, presbyterial, congregational, or self-proclaimed in the consciousness of a divine call: they would all be satisfactory if their weaknesses and failings were not so evident.

And those who warn against the dangers of a "superchurch" must be heeded. A united Church in each city, in each nation, and throughout the world will consist of sinful men, and they will be prone to abuse whatever power is placed in their hands. A united Church will consist of men who are not perfectly wise, and they will be prone to overorganize and to waste their resources. A united Church will consist of people who have a good opinion of themselves, and they will be tempted to draw unchristian lines of distinction between those who are within the fellowship and those who are outside. The separated denominations are doing all these things right now, and the same people can be expected to act the same way in a new setting.

But it is equally true that a church without authority, in which every man did what was right in his own eyes, would still be a church of self-centered, foolish, sinful men. And in their anarchy they would be equally disloyal to Christ and obstructive of his saving mission. A mob is sometimes controlled by a demon of power even when it thinks itself to be unorganized.

Hence, it would seem to be important to assure that a united Church will not be too tightly organized; indeed, to assure that it will preserve some of the advantages of competition and criticism that exist in the denominational situation. It would be questionable for it to have only one huge publishing house when it could have a half-dozen or more in one country, meeting the varied needs and interests of its members. The same applies to church school curricula, to missionary and social enterprise, to theological education, and to all the rest of the spectrum of church administration.

As of today, we really do not know what the structure of a united Church would be like. A certain pattern is emerging among those who are discussing union, mainly among Anglicans, Methodists, and churches in the Calvinist tradition, but bringing these churches together would be only a small beginning in the great task of Christian reunion. The Lutherans have not yet become a part of the picture, nor have the Eastern Orthodox Churches. And even if all these were to come together in one fellowship, the Roman Catholic Church would still have its centrally important part to play in the work of reunion.

But we do know, as the Epistle to the Ephesians puts it, that we all share one Lord, one faith, one baptism, and one God and Father of all. We have begun to recapture an awareness of the fact that we are one body with one Spirit. And we have every reason to trust that one Spirit to lead us into all truth. Actually, we do not have to know the precise details of the goal to which he is leading us. All that we need to know is the next step.

A famous chess player was asked how many moves ahead he planned. His answer was: "Just one; but I try to make that move a good one." So, in ecumenical thinking and dialogue, all we have to do is make one good move at a time.

And one way to tell whether our moves are good ones is to test them by their relevance to the mission of the Church. Do they liberate persons, congregations, and institutions to act lovingly, redemptively, and effectively in the worship of God and in service to his people? If so, they are moves in the direction in which God is calling us to go.

As churches grow toward unity, members of religiously divided families will have the opportunity to share again in the deepest things of life. Local churches will, in the vast majority of cases, continue as separate congregations; but they will be able to work together more freely, and if obedience to their mission dictates that they become one congregation, there will be no denominational barrier standing in their way. In dozens of other ways, Christian unity will give all of us the freedom to do things we would like to do, and things we know we ought to do, but cannot do today.

Unity when Christ wills it, and in the way that Christ wills it—this was the formulation of the Abbe Couturier, a Roman Catholic ecumenist of the difficult years before Pope John, and it epitomizes the spirit in which we must continue to pray and work today.

> *O Lord Jesus Christ, who said to your disciples, "Peace I leave with you, my peace I give to you," take account not of our sins, but the faith of your Church; and grant to it that peace and unity which is according to your will.*

III

"The One Apostolic Faith"

The New Delhi statement on church unity speaks of "one fully committed fellowship, holding the one apostolic faith, preaching the one Gospel." It is into this fellowship that a man comes by baptism and confession of Jesus Christ as Lord and Saviour.

This affirmation is a reminder that basically the Church of Christ is not a truth-seeking society, but a truth-proclaiming society, or more accurately, perhaps, a good-news-reporting society. It exists to tell people about what God has done, is doing, and will do for man's salvation. Of course, a great deal of truth-seeking goes on within the Church, for Christians are insatiably interested in finding out everything they can about God and man and the things visible and invisible of God's creation. Even the central message of the gospel must be pondered over, analyzed, and more deeply understood and expressed in every generation in images meaningful to that generation. Nevertheless, the Church's essential reason for existence is "that we may declare the wonderful deeds of him who called us out of darkness into his marvellous light."

In the sixteenth century, Christians fell into division over a number of theological issues which seemed to all concerned to lie close to the heart of their faith. People differed not only over the issues themselves, but also over the authority to which such issues were to be referred. The Scriptures alone? Or the Scriptures plus the Tradition—the ongoing life and self-understanding of the Church?

In *Principles of Church Union,* the Consultation on Church Union has made a notable contribution to the ending of this four-hundred-year-old controversy about Scripture and Tradition. This is significant because of the place Tradition plays in the life of one of the nine churches (the Episcopal). But it is even more significant in relation to the greater task of finding common ground with the Roman Catholic and Eastern Orthodox Christians of the world, as we pray and work for the unity of all the people of God.

Pointing out that the New Testament itself was the product of the living Christian Tradition, the chapter on "The Faith of the Church" says (*Principles of Church Union,* p. 22), "By Tradition we understand the whole life of the Church ever guided and nourished by the Holy Spirit, and expressed in its worship, witness, way of life, and its order."

The Disciples of Christ came into being about the beginning of the nineteenth century with a conscious rejection of Tradition as an authoritative element in the life of the Church. One of their representatives at the Oberlin, Ohio, meeting of the Consultation in 1963, remarked: "Our authority was to be the Scriptures, and the Scriptures alone. But almost as soon as we became organized we found we had to divide into two Churches—because we had two different traditions of understanding the Scriptures." The practical issue was over the use of organs in churches, which some thought entirely in accord with the Bible and others thought entirely unwarranted by the Bible.

The report of the Oberlin meeting went on to say: "The members of the Consultation are aware that we are confronted not only by Scripture and Tradition (understood as the whole life of the Church) but also by Scripture, Tradition and the traditions—those individual expressions of the Tradition which more or less characterize particular churches and those customs of the churches which have arisen in various times and places. We have no doubt that such tradition must ever be brought under the judgment of the Scriptures." *

It might have been added that in ecumenical encounter the churches can enrich their own life from the contributions of other Christian traditions. To recognize the genuineness of other forms of Christian experience is a gift from which many blessings will flow. They too are a part of the whole life of the Church.

A similar assertion of the vital relationship between Scripture and Tradition was made in the report of the Fourth World Conference on Faith and Order of the World Council of Churches at Montreal in 1963, a few months after the Oberlin meeting of the Consultation. The report of Section II of that Conference said:

> . . . We exist as Christians by the Tradition of the Gospel (the *paradosis* of the *kerygma*) testified in Scripture, transmitted in and by the Church through the power of the Holy Spirit. Tradition taken in this sense is actualized in the preaching of the Word, in the administration of the Sacraments and worship, in Christian teaching and theology, and in mission and witness to Christ by the lives of the members of the Church.

> What is transmitted in the process of tradition is the Christian faith, not only as a sum of tenets, but as a living reality transmitted through the operation of the Holy Spirit. We can speak of the Christian Tradition (with a capital T), whose content is

---

* *C.O.C.U.: The Official Reports of the Four Meetings of the Consultation* (Cincinnati: Forward Movement Publications, 1965), p. 25.

God's revelation and self-giving in Christ, present in the life of the Church.

But this Tradition which is the work of the Holy Spirit is embodied in traditions (in the two senses of the word, both as referring to diversity in forms of expression, and in the sense of separate communions). The traditions in Christian history are distinct from, and yet connected with, the Tradition. They are the expressions and manifestations in diverse historical forms of the one truth and reality which is Christ.*

The report then goes on to point out the difficulties of evaluating the faithfulness of the several traditions to the Tradition, especially when they are in conflict with each other. Although all churches appeal to Scripture, they do not always interpret the Scriptures the same way. However, theology and the study of church history are becoming more ecumenical, in the sense that present-day scholars are able to listen to each other and learn from each other, taking a more objective view of their own church's history and traditions; and in this development the report sees great hope for the future. It quotes Santayana: "Those who fail to comprehend their histories are doomed to re-enact them."

The framers of this report represented a wide spectrum of churches—those within the Consultation, and many others, such as the Eastern Orthodox, the Lutherans, the Baptists, the Old Catholics—in thirty-two different countries.

Among contemporary Roman Catholic theologians, the same problem is being discussed, and a similar development is taking place. The Vatican Council, in its Constitution on Divine Revelation, said:†

---

* *The Fourth World Conference on Faith and Order* (New York: Association Press, 1964), p. 52.

† The edition of Vatican II pronouncements used for this and subsequent quotations is that published by the U.S. Catholic Conference, 1312 Massachusetts Avenue, N.W., Washington, D.C. 20005.

There exists a close connection and communication between sacred tradition and sacred Scripture. For both of them, flowing from the same divine wellspring, in a certain way merge into a unity and tend toward the same end. For sacred Scripture is the Word of God inasmuch as it is consigned to writing under the inspiration of the divine Spirit, while sacred tradition takes the Word of God entrusted by Christ the Lord and the Holy Spirit to the Apostles, and hands it on to their successors in its full purity, so that led by the light of the Spirit of truth, they may in proclaiming it preserve this Word of God faithfully, explain it, and make it more widely known. Consequently it is not from sacred Scripture alone that the Church draws her certainty about everything which has been revealed. Therefore both sacred tradition and sacred Scripture are to be accepted and venerated with the same sense of loyalty and reverence.

While this position is not quite the same as that expressed in *Principles of Church Union* and the Faith and Order report, it represents a definite movement of convergence. The old idea of "two sources of revelation" has now become a concept of two inseparable aspects of the way in which the one revelation is conveyed to the world.

When the Vatican Council first took up the subject, the draft presented by the preparatory commission tended very much in the opposite direction—to the concept that some divinely revealed truths are to be found in Scripture and some in Tradition, instead of treating Scripture and Tradition together as concordant witnesses to the Word of God. This draft was rejected by a large majority in the first session of the Council, but not by the two-thirds required for its withdrawal. It was at this point that Pope John XXIII intervened to withdraw the document and thereby showed the assembled bishops that they would have freedom to conduct the Council in their own way.

What is the "one apostolic faith" to which both Scripture and Tradition bears witness? The opening words of *Principles of Church Union* (Preamble, p. 20 of *Consultation on Church Union, 1967*) declare it succinctly: "We affirm our faith in the one God, Father, Son, and Holy Spirit, who has given us our unity in the one, holy, catholic, and apostolic Church." But this faith is set out more fully in the chapter on "The Faith of the Church," in the context of the Bible.

The united Church acknowledges that the Holy Scriptures of the Old and New Testaments have a unique authority. They witness to God's revelation, fulfilled in Jesus Christ, and to man's response to the divine revelation. They testify to God's mighty acts of creation and recreation, judgment and mercy; they declare God's saving purpose; they proclaim the gospel which is the power of God for salvation; they point to the glorious consummation of his Kingdom, which has no end. They are the inspired writings which bear witness to the divine deeds in our history by which God has called into being and sustained his people and by which God calls all men to unite in his service and share in his reconciliation of the world to himself.

Jesus Christ, crucified and risen, the living Lord and head of the Church, is the center of the Holy Scriptures. . . .

This statement on the Scriptures might be useful for any contemporary Christian who is asked by an inquiring friend what part the Bible plays in his life. Of course, many more things could be said about the Bible and its contents, and perhaps a clause ought to be inserted on the Scriptures as the Word of God expressed in the words of men.*

Nevertheless, as a strong and forthright statement of what

---

* As the Vatican Decree puts it, "However, since God speaks in sacred Scripture through men in human fashion, the interpreter of sacred Scripture, in order to see clearly what God wanted to communicate to us, should carefully investigate what meaning the sacred writers really intended, and what God wanted to manifest by means of their words" (Chapter III, No. 12).

the Bible means to Christians after a hundred years or more of historical and literary criticism of the sacred writings, this paragraph of *Principles of Church Union* is an ecumenical achievement. On this point, present-day Christians can agree with each other more than they agree with archaic formal statements of their own churches.

The nine churches involved in C.O.C.U. have had varied attitudes toward creedal statements summing up the Christian faith. The Disciples held as a founding principle that the New Testament should speak for itself on the faith of the Church. Any other creed, being man-made, would be without authority and possibly harmful. In this they were rebelling against the detailed Confessions of Faith of the older churches of the Reformation which attempted to set out a complete exposition of "the system of doctrine taught in Holy Scriptures." The two Presbyterian churches in the Consultation are representatives of this confessional tradition. The former Congregationalists within the United Church of Christ have gone through an evolution from early confessionalism to recent anti-confessionalism. The Episcopalians rely on the two ancient Creeds, the Apostles' and Nicene, and refer other doctrinal issues to the Book of Common Prayer, on the principle that "the rule for praying is the rule for believing." The Methodists have a common doctrinal history with the Episcopalians, but their overwhelming emphasis has been on personal relationships rather than doctrinal agreement. The "Articles of Religion" of the Methodists and the Episcopalians agree in most matters word for word (the former being a revision of the latter), but neither Church makes much use of them.

It would seem that the bringing together of these conflicting traditions would be an impossible enterprise, but there are reasons for optimism. First, the work of the Consultation over the past six years has shown a remarkable degree of agreement on the basic content of the faith of the Church. Tomorrow's Church believes in a living God, a crucified and risen Christ, a life-giving Spirit. It accepts the witness of the Scriptures to the mighty acts of God in history for our salvation. It looks forward to the culmination of history in a divine consummation and the gift of everlasting life.

The radical theologies which make headlines in the popular magazines, proposing that the doctrine of the Trinity be jettisoned, or announcing the death of God, have not made the slightest dent in this faith. There is a constructive element in this radical theologizing which the Church must appropriate. This is the truth that man has entered a new civilization in the technological and other revolutions of our times, a world in which human powers for good or ill are unlike anything that has been known before. We have to cultivate new virtues and wrestle against new sins—or perhaps newly devastating consequences of old sins, such as national pride and racial prejudice. And the relationships between Christians and non-Christians must be scrutinized in terms of the same opportunities and dangers. However, the Father, Son, and Holy Spirit in whom we believe are more than equal to the task of being the God of this new world. It is God's world just as the old worlds of other upheavals and revolutions remained God's world.

A second reason for optimism is that, as an agreement on the authority of the Bible can be found and stated, it may well be that, although we come from many different traditions about statements of faith, we are all living as Christians in a time and place to which our faith has to be proclaimed basically in the same way.

The question of "Confession of Faith in Union Negotiations" has been superbly treated by J. D. McCaughey, an Australian Presbyterian, in an address to the international

Consultation on Church Union Negotiations at Bossey in 1967.* His main points were as follows:

1. *To confess the Christian Faith is to acknowledge that there is a Christian message. . . .* Churches entering into union should be concerned that the Christian message will be heard in each generation. That is their primary concern. The preservation of right doctrine should serve that end: it is not an end in itself. The Church does not exist to preserve a body of teaching but to bring men into a new relationship of faith in God through Jesus Christ, and this comes through the preached message, the Word. . . .

2. *The Confession will point to the Scriptures as containing the texts from which the Church preaches. . . .* [As a result of modern critical study] the Biblical documents in their several settings have come alive. Gone is the old abstracting of doctrinal or ethical truths, which can be drawn out in such a way that dogmaticians or moralists can take the crude statement and with the aid of Greek philosophy or Roman morals build an edifice of Christian truth. In its place we have released apostolic mouthpieces or mentors speaking about the controversy in which they find themselves engaged with God and His people. On the axis of that controversy, a controversy breaks through to our imagination: we find ourselves being engaged, and the issue of faith or unbelief, of obedience or disobedience is precipitated into our lives. . . .

3. *The Sacraments.* The next place to which a united church will point men for the renewal of faith and life is of course the Sacraments—of Baptism and the Lord's Supper. Again we should be concerned less with the quasi-philosophical and theological definition of their nature, and more about their use. He who does this will come to know the doctrine. . . .

The story is told of a Jewish woman converted to Christianity, who was asked at the end of her period of instruction if she understood the significance of the sacraments. She answered, "How can I know until I have received them?" The Church will come to understand the Sacraments—their mystery—as she lives more fully by them. A basis of union should be a commitment to

* *Midstream,* Vol. VI, No. 9, pp. 23 ff.

live together more fully the sacramental life, to do so with more discipline, a going in the way of discipleship, not the imposed discipline of legal requirement and enactment which in this sphere achieves so little. . . .

4. *The Classical Creeds of Christendom.* The fourth direction to which the uniting churches will together point in order that faith may be renewed is to the classical creeds of the Christian Church, certainly the Apostles' Creed and the so-called Nicene Creed; and possibly also the Christological formulations of Chalcedon. . . . The Creeds can no longer be used as "tests of orthodoxy" for individual members, as some so frightenedly see them. In spite of the "I" form, creeds are not primarily individual expressions of faith: they articulate the faith of the Church. . . . It must be made clear that the function of creeds in the life of the Church is not to damage men's consciences or to blunt their sensibilities. . . .

For what purpose and in what manner are they to be understood? Whatever their original uses, creeds have become acts of the Church's worship or (in F. D. Maurice's phrase) "acts of affiance." The Church declares the name of the One to whom she belongs. The individual worshipper is asked to enter into this worshipping, confessing fellowship. In so doing he is not asked *ex animo* to make every clause his own; he is asked to say, in effect: "I believe in, I put my confidence in the One who in the Christian tradition (as distinct from other traditions) is described in these ways. I wish to belong to Christ and His people who for centuries have used this language."

5. *The Confessions of the Reformation.* [These] mark the way we have come. Properly understood they point to the fellowship of men and women to whom we would belong and who were sustained by faith. . . . But it would be intolerable to be asked to believe that the Holy Spirit only guided the Church (a) to recognize the canon of Scripture; and (b) to leave us some confessional documents of the 16th and 17th centuries. He is a living personal presence. . . .

In union, it is to be hoped that we shall be willing to express our indebtedness to the many witnesses of the Church of the ages.

The danger lies in one Confession which is either neglected or idolized. In this, as in some other matters, there is safety in numbers.

None of the churches engaged in the Consultation is given to heresy-hunting. In today's world, to invoke penalties for erroneous belief casts doubt on the soundness of a belief that has to be defended by such means. Yet, the Nicene Creed, in particular, is the common affirmation of faith of more than 90 per cent of the Christians of the world—the Roman Catholics, the Eastern Orthodox, the Lutherans, the Anglicans, the Reformed Churches. Professor McCaughey is right in underlining the significance of these classical statements of Christian faith, as expressing the Church's unity in faith, both in space and in time.

The passages in the Creeds with which some Christians have difficulties—for example, the assumption of a three-story universe of heaven, earth, and hell—are solidly based on Scripture, and like the Scriptures themselves their language and imagery needs at times to be understood metaphorically, as presenting reality in symbols which should not be pressed with heavy literalness. Contemporary Christians allow for this automatically when they read the Bible, and creedal Christians do so equally automatically when they recite the Creed.

At its 1968 meeting in Dayton, Ohio, the Consultation adopted a statement attempting to meet this problem, as follows:

In that portion of the Plan of Union dealing with the faith of the Church, we need to recognize (1) the historically conditioned character of the creeds; (2) the corporate character of the historic creeds; and (3) the principle that the creeds are for the guidance of the members of the church and are to be used persuasively and not coercively.

Several of the churches in the Consultation have recently produced statements of their faith that are worthy of attention. The most comprehensive of these is the United Presbyterian Book of Confessions, adopted in 1967. It includes, first, the Nicene Creed, in its proper form of "we believe" (as it was first written down at the Council of Constantinople, A.D. 381); second, the Apostles' Creed; then, a series of historic confessions of faith of Reformation times: and finally, the Confession of 1967 (see Appendix, p. 167), which begins with a statement subjecting all such confessions to the authority of Jesus Christ and denying them exclusive validity or irreformability. This new Confession is an attempt to say what it is important for the Church to say to the world in these times.

A briefer statement, but one with special intensity of meaning because it was, so to speak, the marriage vow of the United Church of Christ, is that Church's statement of faith, adopted at the Synod of 1959, the first after the 1957 Synod which adopted the act of union. An accompanying note (printed, with the statement itself, in Appendix, p. 152) says, "For some of us, it is not too much to say, the United Church of Christ really began that day as we confessed our faith together and spontaneously sang the Doxology."

A modern English translation of the Nicene Creed, also using the plural form and dropping the words "and the son" in the passage referring to the Holy Spirit has been included in a Communion service approved for trial use in the Episcopal Church. The words omitted were not in the original Creed, and are an obstacle to relations between the Eastern Orthodox, who do not use them, and Western Christians who do.

So far, we have been discussing the faith of the *Church*— the witness which the Christian fellowship makes corporately to the mighty acts of God "for us men and our salvation."

But *Principles of Church Union* rightly makes the starting point of its chapter on "The Faith of the Church" a deeper meaning of the word "faith"—personal commitment to, and trust in, Jesus Christ as Lord and Saviour. As the chapter says, "Only by costly, individual choice can men and women yield full loyalty, trust and fealty to Jesus Christ; and it is only by his grace that we become members of his Body. Corporate confessions are intended to guard, encourage, elicit, guide and direct this personal commitment, not to coerce or control it, nor substitute a corporate act for it."

Thus, "The Faith of the Church" begins, as does the New Delhi statement, with all in each place "who are baptised into Jesus Christ and confess him as Lord and Saviour."

To do this is to become a "member" of the Church, and the united Church will regard as its members those who are members of any of the uniting churches. But to be a member is not intended to convey the idea of joining a club for a year or so, at one's personal convenience. Rather, in St. Paul's image, it is to become an organic part of a living body—the Body of Christ.

The dynamic relationship between the faith of the member and the faith of the body—between faith and *the* faith is well stated: "The united Church will recognize that the Head of the Body has made it steward and trustee of the truth of the Gospel. It will seek to discharge its responsibility under God, as the corporate guardian and teacher of the faith within which each Christian makes his own offering of himself, to communicate understanding of the faith to every member, and to help him put that faith to work. . . . Each Christian's witness to the faith indeed remains personal. But the faith is loyalty, individual and corporate, to the Lord who wills to be acknowledged as sovereign ruler of the world."

Grant, Almighty Father, that your Church, built upon the foundation of the Apostles and Prophets with Christ Jesus himself as the cornerstone, may be joined together in unity of spirit by their doctrine and made a holy temple acceptable to you; through the same Jesus Christ our Lord. Amen.

IV

"Joining in Common Prayer"

The worship of God is the first, and the only permanent, business of the Church. Christians down through the centuries have joined in spirit with the author of the book of Revelation in singing. "Worthy art thou, our Lord and God, to receive glory and honor and power, for thou didst create all things, and by thy will they existed and were created."

Even though Christians agree on the centrality of worship, the varieties of ways of worship present real problems for churches that are seeking to unite. For many lay people, the possibility of being confronted with a different pattern of worship is the principal stumbling block to union.

Those engaged in making plans for church union try to take account of these difficulties, but perhaps church leaders do not, as a group, share the intensity of feeling of many lay people on the subject. Their ecumenical experience and reflection has given them a perspective which makes it easier for them to sense the basic unity underlying the various forms of worship and to enter heartily and freely into unfamiliar patterns.

Professor K. Grayston, of the Methodist Church of England,

issued a needed reminder to church leaders in an address to the Bossey Consultation on Church Union Negotiations. He said: "When churches discuss reunion they are proposing to bring together in one community Christians with different kinds of spirituality and church order. It is important to recognize that spirituality and church order are not beliefs that people can discard or modify at will. This is their way of being Christian. It needs a great imaginative leap, which can be prompted by love, grace, and holiness, for most Christians to accept for themselves another type of spirituality and church order as a genuine Christian experience." *

He had previously defined "spirituality" as follows: "I mean your particular way of believing in God—the picture you have in mind when you think of him spontaneously, not when you are trying to remember what somebody taught you; the God you address in an unspoken prayer of entreaty or joy when you experience anxiety or unexpected pleasure. In the word spirituality I include the kind of certainty you have in holding on to God, the conviction behind your religion, the authority you can rely on when your own faith is shaken, the expectation you have when you go to worship, the carry-over of your Sunday piety into weekday living, and the resources in your tradition for extending your spiritual grasp and for growing in grace."

The Consultation on Church Union recognizes both the validity of these different styles of spirituality and the tenaciousness of church people in holding on to them. Indeed, those who live out their particular kind of church life fully and deeply are the most important contribution of each church to the others.

Consultation on Church Union, 1967, in a chapter on

* *Midstream,* Vol. VI, No. 3, pp. 47 ff.

"Stages and Steps toward a United Church," proposed that unification be a gradual process, a growing together, rather than merely the adoption by governing bodies of a series of resolutions intended to pick up 25 million people from one place and set them down in another. After agreement on the essentials of faith, worship, sacraments, and ministry, and adoption of a plan of union, it would be possible to unify ministry and membership in such a way that any minister and any member would be welcome in any of the nine churches. They would, under the guidance of a provisional council, plan all their new work together. But they would continue for a time under their familiar forms of worship and church order before the final stage of full unification under an agreed constitution.

The chapter says, "We do indeed feel that a better and wiser constitution can be written after a period of experience in unity, for we shall then have had the chance which only time can give to solve small problems, learn other ways, discover one another, lose suspicions, and gain a sense of the single mission which commands us all—gifts we must have if the Constitution is to be any thing save a safeguard of compromise and prejudice."

However, a committee working on proposals for the structure of a united Church moved somewhat away from this position in its report to the 1968 meeting. Unification of ministries—*i.e.,* the adoption of the episcopate by the churches which do not now have it—was found to be almost an impossibility without major changes in their constitutional structures, and it was doubted that they would be willing to make such changes for anything less than a complete and final union in which each participating church would surrender its legislative authority to a central body. If there is to be a process of growing together, it will have to take place before unification, according to the thinking at the Dayton meeting. Since all reports adopted at Dayton were of a tentative character, it remains to be seen whether this position or the earlier Dallas-Cambridge position will prevail.

In the chapter on "The Worship of the Church," the Consultation makes use of insights into the nature of Christian worship which have developed from contemporary liturgical studies. The word "liturgy" is derived from a Greek word meaning "the people's work" or "public duty," and in present usage it means the whole cycle of the Church's public worship. Roman Catholics, Lutherans, Episcopalians, Presbyterians, Methodists, and others have developed a common body of liturgical understanding which can almost be described as an ecumenical movement behind the ecumenical movement. Scholars and pastors have arrived at profound agreement on the dynamics of worship and the general pattern that best expresses these dynamics.

"The sacramental rites of baptism and communion are at the heart of the Church's worship, being commanded by the Lord and uniquely expressive of the root relationships between man and God," the Consultation says. Here again, the New Delhi statement on the nature of unity is fulfilled, as those who are baptized form one fellowship, "preaching the one Gospel, breaking the one bread, joining in common prayer, and reaching out in witness and service to all."

This does not mean that every church service has to be a Communion service (although both the Disciples of Christ and the Episcopalians think it important to celebrate "the Lord's Service on the Lord's day"). But it does mean that other services are to be seen within the context of these two supreme actions in which men surrender themselves to God and God gives himself to men.

So, *the* liturgy of the Church is not complete without the

coming together in Communion of the fellowship of the baptized. Other services are parts of this total liturgy.

It is impossible, moreover, to separate liturgy and life. The Consultation includes in worship "every sincere act of loving response to God, individual or corporate, elaborate or simple, private or public, in the congregation or in the world." For our lives are what we offer to God in our worship, in union with Christ, and our worship must be both our motive power and our marching orders for daily living. This principle is older than Christianity. "What does the LORD require of you but to do justice, and to love kindness, and to walk humbly with your God?" says the prophet Micah (6:8). Christ himself enjoins us to leave our gift before the altar and go and be reconciled to our brother before offering it (Matthew 5:24).

It is interesting to note the parallels of some themes of the Consultation's chapter on worship with themes of the Constitution on the Liturgy adopted by the Vatican Council.

The Sacraments and the connection between liturgy and life, referred to above, are thus described in the Roman Catholic statement: "The liturgy . . . moves the faithful, filled with the paschal sacraments, to be one in holiness; it prays 'that they may hold fast in their lives to what they have grasped by their faith'; the renewal in the Eucharist of the covenant between the Lord and man draws the faithful into the compelling love of Christ and sets them on fire. From the liturgy, therefore, and especially from the Eucharist, as from a fount, grace is poured forth upon us; and the sanctification of men in Christ and the glorification of God, to which all the other activities of the Church are directed as toward their end, is achieved in the most efficacious possible way."

Reading from the Scriptures. The Consultation: "We hold it to be the right and duty of Christians, expressive of their humble dependence on the Word of God, to hear the words of

Scripture, in appropriate order and manner, as an act of worship in itself, as well as to serve the ministry of teaching and preaching." The Council: "Sacred Scripture is of the greatest importance in the celebration of the liturgy. For it is from Scripture that lessons are read and explained in the homily, and psalms are sung; the prayers, collects, and liturgical songs are scriptural in their inspiration, and it is from the Scriptures that actions and signs derive their meaning."

Preaching. The Consultation: "The preaching of the Word of God is an essential element in every form of public worship, save for urgent cause. As part of the normal order of public worship, the following functions of preaching may be particularly set down: To identify and describe the acts of God, whether recorded in Scripture read at the service, or apparent in some other way; to aid the congregation to see and receive the gifts of God in Christ; to stimulate their obedient witness; to keep the forms and acts of worship themselves open to the cleansing judgment of God. . . ." The Council: "Because the sermon is part of the liturgical service, the best place for it is to be indicated in the rubrics, as far as the nature of the rite will allow; the ministry of preaching is to be fulfilled with exactitude and fidelity. The sermon, moreover, should draw its content mainly from scriptural and liturgical sources, and its character should be that of a proclamation of God's wonderful works in the history of salvation. . . ."

Informal Prayer. The Consultation: "For the privilege of offering its public prayers to God, the united church will have for use the wealth of differing traditions, ranging from free prayer to formal, fully ordered services." The Council: "Bible services should be encouraged, especially on the vigils of the more solemn feasts, on some weekdays in Advent and Lent, and on Sundays and feast days. They are particularly to be commended in places where no priest is available; when this is so, a deacon or some other persons authorized by the bishop should preside over the celebration."

Congregational Participation. The Consultation: "By means of unison readings, responsive readings, hymns, versicles, litanies, and other such forms, the members of the congregation will have the opportunity and responsibility for sharing actively in corporate worship." The Council: "To promote active participation, the people should be encouraged to take part by means of acclamations, responses, psalmody, antiphons, and songs, as well as by actions, gestures, and bodily attitudes. And at the proper times all should observe a reverent silence" [a good Quaker point that the Consultation missed].

Music. The Consultation: "It will be the intention of the united church to encourage maximum and proper use of hymns and music in the life of the church. To this end, each congregation will be encouraged to explore and use the hymnody and music of the entire Church." The Council: "Religious singing by the people is to be skillfully fostered, so that in devotions and sacred exercises, as also during liturgical services, the voices of the faithful may ring out." And "In certain parts of the world, especially mission lands, there are peoples who have their own musical traditions and these play a great part in their religious and social life. For this reason, due importance is to be attached to their music, and a suitable place is to be given to it, not only in forming their attitude toward religion, but also in adapting worship to their native genius. . . ."

In some of these common emphases, the Consultation might be thought to be imitating the Roman Catholics, but in others the influence appears to be in the opposite direction. Actually, what is represented here is not imitation of one by another but, rather, the development of a common store of liturgical knowledge and understanding.

The Church year is a central element in the worship of some of the churches in the Consultation, but not in others. In the Episcopal Church, not only are the major seasons and the feasts of our Lord and the Apostles observed but also a supplemental list of saints' days, which has been authorized for trial use, with appropriate prayers and Bible readings.

In Reformation times, Protestants felt that the role of the saints in the life of the medieval Church was overstressed and they reacted against it with varying degrees of severity. The Consultation apparently is willing to see a great deal of variety on this subject in a united Church.

A Russian Orthodox Church calendar, which has recently come to the author's desk, indicates how such observances can be one of the "fun" parts of religion. Not only are Moses and the Old Testament prophets remembered, but many New Testament saints and sinners, such as Zacchaeus, the publican, along with such interesting postbiblical personages and events as: Maxim of Totnia, the Fool-in-Christ; John the Hut Dweller; the miraculous appearance of the Ikon of the Mother of God at Kazan; Hermylus, Deacon, and his friend Strautonicus; Cyrus and John, unmercenary doctors; Paul the Simpleminded; John the Silent; Third Finding of the Head of St. John the Baptist; Stephen, Prince of Serbia, and His Mother Militza. Such a calendar almost amounts to a Christian family album, packed with mementos of beloved forebears and memorable events.

The chapter on worship does not take up the issue of "Invocation of saints"—the practice of asking the saints for their assistance, whether in matters practical or spiritual. This is a well-established custom in Roman Catholicism and Eastern Orthodoxy, and is unofficially practiced in many parishes of the Episcopal Church. It is possible for this type of devotion to obscure the truth that we have direct access to God through

Jesus Christ, or to result in our giving to men the honor that is due only to God. But it is also possible for it to give us a lively awareness of the reality of the whole Christian fellowship in time and space, a community in which every member may reach out to help any other member. Presumably, this also is the kind of area in which tomorrow's Church will provide for variety of practice.

A much more central issue is the issue of prayers of petition and intercession in the worship of the Church itself. In a call to worship in the services of Morning and Evening Prayer, the Book of Common Prayer says: ". . . we assemble and meet together to render thanks for the great benefits we have received at his hands, to set forth his most worthy praise, to hear his most holy Word, and to ask those things which are requisite and necessary, as well for the body as the soul." Asking for such needs, both for ourselves and for others, is an important dimension of the Christian life. It is a part of the inner strength of the Pentecostal movement which has swept over the world in our century, and it is one of the reiterated themes in the preaching of Jesus: "Ask, and it will be given you; seek and you will find; knock, and it will be opened to you" (Matthew 7:7). Indeed, the trust which impels us to offer such prayers to our heavenly Father is a part of our praise of his goodness.

The five main themes of prayer are well summarized in the Book of Church Order of the Presbyterian Church in the U.S. (Southern Presbyterian)* in terms which are characteristic of the central Tradition of the Holy Catholic Church:

In *Adoration* the people are to adore the glory and perfection of God as they are made known in his works of creation and providence, in the clear and full revelation he has made in Jesus Christ, and in the work of the Holy Spirit.

* Sec. 206-6. Used by permission.

In *Thanksgiving* the people are to offer gratitude and praise to God for all his mercies, general and particular, spiritual and temporal; above all, for Christ Jesus, Savior and Lord, and for the life eternal which is in him.

In *Confession* the people are humbly to acknowledge unto God their sinfulness in nature and in act, and their sins both of omission and of commission, with a deep sense of the evil of all sin committed against God, our neighbor, and ourselves. They shall ask forgiveness through Jesus Christ. The confession should be concluded by the minister's affirming the assurance of pardon through Jesus Christ as promised in Holy Scripture.

In *Supplication* the people are to ask earnestly through Jesus Christ for the outpouring of the Holy Spirit, for peace with God accompanied by all the fruits of that peace, for abundant supplies of the grace necessary to enable them to be obedient unto God, for support and comfort under trials, and for needed temporal blessings.

In *Intercession* the people are to offer petition on behalf of others; for the visible kingdom of Christ, his Church Universal; for the interest and welfare of human society; and for all to whom God has given civil authority.

The next section (206-7) is also a useful reminder: "The prayer which Christ taught his disciples should be used in the public prayers of the congregation." In some churches that are accustomed to freer forms of worship, the people may go a long time without having the opportunity to use the Lord's Prayer, although it is a central element in what Dr. Grayston called the "spirituality" of other Christian communions.

Variety certainly will, and certainly should, characterize the life of a united Church. Different congregations will undoubtedly maintain different traditions about particulars of worship, vestments, musical taste, and ceremony. Every authentic way of approaching the Lord in adoration, thanksgiving, confession, supplication, and intercession in the Eucharistic fellowship of the baptized has its place in the treasury of the kingdom of God. Yet, variety must be balanced by an equally authentic sense of commitment to each other. Our prayer must be genuinely "common," as the New Delhi statement says: the expression of being all "with one accord in one place," like the apostolic band at Pentecost. Among our human diversities we must also find ways of experiencing our human unity as children of one Father.

The worship of the Church is the heart of the matter—the heart of our life in Christ and the heart of our disunity as well. Facing the threat of radical alteration of his accustomed ways and forms, the devout Christian is tempted to retreat again to the subterfuge of talking about "spiritual unity"—a unity so "spiritual" that those who possess it must maintain separate establishments for expressing it, and must confess themselves unable to enter sincerely and wholeheartedly into common prayer.

There has to be something wrong with a concept of our life in Christ which shuts us out so adamantly from participation with others of his people at the heart of our communion with him. And his prophecy, "there shall be one flock, one shepherd" (John 10:16), encourages us to believe that he will find the way to reconcile us.

> *Grant, we beseech you, merciful God, that your Church, being gathered together in unity by the Holy Spirit, may manifest your power among all peoples, to the glory of your name; through Jesus Christ our Lord, who lives and reigns with you and the same Spirit, from age to age. Amen.*

V

"Baptized into Jesus Christ"

In its chapter on "The Sacraments of the Church," the Consultation on Church Union has made an important contribution to the recovery of the central Christian Tradition. While problems of sacramental doctrine and practice remain, the agreed statements on baptism and Holy Communion provide a solid foundation for further progress.

Through baptism God engrafts the individual person into his people as a living member of the body of Christ. It is a divine symbol, ordinance, sacrament, and mystery, and forms the visible basis of our unity in Jesus Christ. Since it is an act of God in Christ and the sign of our entrance into the whole Church, baptism is to be administered only once.

Through this act of cleansing we are born again of water and spirit, knowing ourselves to be taken up into God's plan of spirit, . . . knowing ourselves to be taken up into God's plan of

Such language moves the nine churches in the Consultation toward unity not only with each other but also with the historic churches of East and West, the Orthodox and the Roman Catholics. The sacrament is seen as "an act of God in Christ," and in later paragraphs as "a decisive work of God" and "an act of Christ in his Church."

One of the fundamental issues of Reformation times was the degree of emphasis to be given to the concepts of "Christ in his Church" and "Christ over his Church." The Catholic emphasis saw Christ acting in the actions of the Church—in its sacraments, its ministry, its prayers, its decisions on matters of doctrine and discipline. The Protestant emphasis, directed at recalling a prodigal Church to purer faith and purer living, saw the Church under Christ's judgment and in need of reforms which the hierarchy was unwilling to make.

A united Church which seeks to be truly Catholic, truly evangelical, and truly reformed must hold both of these emphases in balance. The Church is indeed Christ's body, the means by which he acts in the world to bring men into union with their heavenly Father and with each other; but the members of that body from the least to the greatest are human beings, constantly falling into sin, misusing his gifts, and misunderstanding his gospel.

Accordingly, Protestantism has historically insisted that there is nothing a man can do to save his soul except to have a lively personal faith in Jesus Christ. The Scriptures are clear that repentance and faith are essential elements of baptism, for it is not a magical act turning a disbeliever into a believer. But they are also clear that for those who come in faith the church's baptismal act is God's act (John 3:5-6; Acts 2:38-39).

In the theological and philosophical language of an earlier day the grace of God in the sacraments was sometimes thought of in mechanical terms, as a fluid flowing through a conduit; or in physical terms, as the functioning of the parts of a body. Such analogies cannot fully describe God's relations with men. More appropriate, at least to contemporary minds, is an analogy drawn from relations between persons. What a man means by a handshake and a word of greeting; what he means by sitting down to dinner with someone; what he means by taking a child in his arms—these are sacramental meanings of actions between human beings. And they help us to understand what Christ means by the actions he instituted in his Church to incorporate men into his kingdom and to nourish them in his life. God's sacraments are more than human actions, conveying gifts beyond the power of men to give; but they are as free and as personal in their nature as the dealings of man with man, and they do not bind God to deal with men only in that particular way. (See the report of a conference of Anglicans and Roman Catholics in Southwark, England, Appendix, p. 182.)

Hence, the fact that Quakers, for example, do not practice baptism or celebrate the Holy Communion does not force us to ignore the reality and depth of their Christian life. We can rejoice that God has brought them into relation with himself by a different way while continuing to believe that the means Christ instituted in the gospel are those he intends most of us to use. Even the Scholastic theologians of the medieval period recognized that God sometimes gives the grace of baptism to those who have not gone through the sacramental action, in the baptism of blood (martyrdom) or the baptism of desire. As St. Peter said (Acts 10:34): "Truly I perceive that God shows no partiality, but in every nation any one who fears him and does what is right is acceptable to him." But, as the story of Cornelius the centurion goes on to relate, the next step for Cornelius and his family was baptism!

Among the churches within the Consultation, the most conspicuous difference in baptismal practice is that, while most of the churches practice infant baptism, one, the Disciples of Christ, practices only adult or, more accurately, believer's baptism. For a Disciple, baptism must be the result of a conscious commitment to faith in Christ by the person being baptized, and immersion must be the mode of baptism. The other churches believe that the young children of a Christian family may be vouched for, or sponsored, by the Christian community of which they are a part, and that pouring or sprinkling may be used instead of immersion. Baptism of infants implies a promise that the child will be brought up in the faith of Jesus Christ, and it would be wrong to baptize a child without reasonable assurance that this will happen.

Principles of Church Union proposes that both types of baptism be allowed, but that baptism be administered only once to any one person.

Actually, such variety of practice was generally accepted in the early days of the Christian Church. Some people were baptized in infancy, some as adults. Those who preferred to delay baptism—sometimes until old age—were acutely conscious of the enormity of postbaptismal sin, as mentioned in the Epistle to the Hebrews (10:26). Those who urged baptism in early infancy were keenly aware of the importance of baptism for participation in Christ's kingdom. Perhaps contemporary American Christians can learn something from the Church of the earlier centuries in fearing the condition of alienation from God which is the result of sin.

This section of *Principles of Church Union* is an abridgement of a longer report adopted at the Princeton, N.J., meeting in 1964. The earlier statement showed more clearly how the two types of baptism, existing side by side, reinforce the united Church's understanding of the full meaning of the sacrament. It said:

Infant baptism is the manifestation of our helplessness and of God's grace on our behalf. It is also a witness to the corporateness of the Christian life. In the nurture of the covenant community it always anticipates confirmation or personal confession of faith. Thereby, parental and congregational vows uttered in behalf of the baptizand are fulfilled. . . .

[In adult baptism] the stress is on the conscious dedication and commitment of awakened faith. By God's gracious act the individual is led to make a responsive decision that involves faithful

obedience to the call of God in Jesus Christ. Since in actual practice adult baptism often follows upon the dedication of the individual in infancy, the witness of the Christian community is used
to prepare and nourish the baptizand in the faith in which he is
baptized.

It appears that a major reason for the differences in practice
is the situation in which the baptismal tradition of a particular
church was formed. The Disciples of Christ, working in rough
and raw frontier settlements, did not experience a stable
Christian community in which young children could be expected as a matter of course to grow up in the faith. And nowadays, in twentieth-century England, where many parents
bring their children to be baptized but never come to church
again until they are carried in, there is a growing group of
Anglican clergy who feel that infant baptism ought to be
abolished!

In Roman Catholicism, Anglicanism, and Eastern Orthodoxy, there is another step in Christian initiation, called
"chrismation" in the East and "confirmation" in the West. This,
too, is regarded as an action of God in his Church, through
the ministry of the bishop or of a priest acting as his deputy
and using oil blessed by him. Though the Episcopal Church
does not use the word "sacrament" for confirmation in its
official formularies (reserving this word for baptism and Holy
Communion), it is generally regarded as one of five lesser sacraments, or sacramental rites.

Confirmation was not originally thought of as intended to
mark the arrival of the Christian at an age for making his
personal profession of faith and "confirming" his baptismal
vows. Rather, the early fathers of the Church saw it as the
"seal of the Holy Spirit," which was given by the Apostles to
Philip's converts in Samaria (Acts 8:14-24). In Ephesians
the seal of the Spirit is described as "the guarantee of our

inheritance until we come into possession of it, to the praise of his glory" (1:14), and in I John 5:8, some scholars see the reference to the three witnesses—"the Spirit, the water, and the blood"—as a reference to the three parts of Christian initiation—chrismation (confirmation), baptism, and first Communion. The order in which they are mentioned is thought to be evidence that in some places confirmation was given before the baptismal immersion; when St. Ambrose refers to this passage he changes the order to "the water, the spirit, and the blood."

The normal procedure in the early days of the Church was to have the new Christian go through the whole rite of entrance into the Christian community at once, whether he was a baby or an adult. This is still basically the practice in the Orthodox Churches. In Western Christendom, however, the scarcity of bishops made this impractical; and little by little confirmation has evolved into a rite of equipping the adolescent Christian for the responsibilities of maturity.

And, as *Principles of Church Union* indicates, this emphasis is a helpful and practical one, bringing out the fact that a mature Christian must be a responsible, personally committed Christian. (For a contrasting proposal, see the Southwark report previously mentioned, Appendix, p. 182.)

While *Principles of Church Union* did not go very far into a discussion of confirmation, the Dayton meeting opened up the subject in a committee report that said:

Confirmation is an act which derives its significance from baptism. By this act members have confirmed to them the promise of God given to them in their baptism; they accept as their own responsibility the vows made in their behalf as children, and are commissioned to go into the world to fulfill their ministry. Confirmation, by prayer with the laying-on of hands of a bishop or presbyter is an effectual sign that God gives the Holy Spirit to each member to fulfill his ministry within the Church and for the world. In the uniting Church confirmation is to be administered to those who affirm that Christ has brought forth in them the response of faith, and whose affirmation is acknowledged by the presbyter and congregation.

In the case of believer's baptism, the candidate, in the presence of the congregation, shall make profession of his faith. The ritual of baptism shall include prayer for the gift of the Holy Spirit, the laying-on of hands by the bishop or presbyter, and the acceptance of the full responsibilities of church membership; and it shall be followed by admission to the Lord's Table.

Throughout the churches today, there is much discussion about the meaning of confirmation and the need for reconsidering its form and intent. The way should be kept open for further exploration of new meanings for this act.

One example of this current rethinking is found in "the Dutch catechism," an exposition of the Catholic faith for adults by the bishops of the Netherlands, published in America under the title *A New Catechism:*

What does it mean, it might be asked, when we say that the Holy Spirit is given at confirmation? Have we not already received the Spirit at baptism?

But there is no contradiction. The gift bestowed in baptism is strengthened in confirmation, which is the "Pentecostal finale" of baptism. Originally confirmation was given soon after baptism, as is still the case in the East. Just as Jesus was anointed by the Spirit just after coming out of the Jordan, and just as he breathed the Spirit upon his disciples soon after rising from the dead (and just as, in fact, people were anointed with perfumes after bathing) so too, after the purifications on which the emphasis is laid at baptism, the joy and strength of the Holy Spirit are celebrated once more very specially at confirmation.*

One of the reasons for our current difficulties in coming to

---

* *A New Catechism* (New York: Herder and Herder, 1967), p. 257. Used by permission.

a clear understanding of the significance of confirmation is that what was generally regarded in the New Testament as one rite of Christian initiation with two focal points—an immersion and an anointing—has become two separate actions separated in time by a period of years. (A reverse development happened in the Lord's Supper, in that two actions, the blessing of bread at the beginning of a meal and wine at the end, were brought together into one action by omitting the meal.)

The Dayton statement does not particularly stress the relationship of confirmation to the ministry of the bishop. Here, Episcopalians feel that they have something to contribute to the life of tomorrow's Church, something meaningful and precious in their own church life.

One not-so-incidental aspect of confirmation by the bishop is its testimony to the fact that the church member is not just a member of a local congregation but of a worldwide Christian fellowship of which the bishop is the representative; one's participation in the life of the whole Church is not complete until it is confirmed, with prayer and the laying on of hands, by the pastor of pastors. This is one of the important ways in which the bishop can serve as "a principal symbol and means of continuity and unity of the Church" (*Principles*, Chapter 4), and establish a personal spiritual relationship with every member of his flock.

Confirmation is sometimes thought of as a sort of ordination to lay ministry, and this too has its value. As in II Timothy 1:6, we are reminded to rekindle the gift of God that is within us through the laying on of apostolic hands, for each adult Christian is a minister of Christ to the world.

The custom in Roman Catholicism and Eastern Orthodoxy of maintaining the bishop's relationship with confirmation even when he delegates his role to a priest, by sending the priest the oil for the purpose, could be meaningfully expressed in other ways. One such way might be giving the confirmand a copy of the Holy Scriptures sent by the bishop, as a visible sign of the involvement of the wider Church in this important spiritual event.

Every church has something to contribute to the double task of recovering the fullness of the Christian Tradition and expressing it in terms which make Christ manifest to today's world. The Disciples' practice of baptism by immersion is certainly such a contribution, for the symbolism of this truly scriptural and ecumenical form of baptism is far better than that of pouring or sprinkling. It is a dying and rising again, a new birth, a self-surrender to Christ in faith—and equally to the point, a full bath, not just a washing of the parts of the body that show. While the other modes are adequate in case of necessity, surely the united Church should commend immersion as the normal mode. However, the Consultation has not seen fit to challenge the member churches on this point.

> *Grant, blessed Lord, that as we are baptized into the death of your Son our Saviour Jesus Christ, so by continually subduing our corrupt affections we may be buried with him and pass through the grave and gate of death to our joyful resurrection; through the self-giving of him who died and was buried and rose again for us, Jesus Christ, your Son and our Lord. Amen.*

VI

"Breaking the One Bread"

The Holy Communion is the central action of the Christian
community. Yet it has also been the subject of bitter controversy, and as the sign of the unity of the Church it has also
served as a sign of division among Christians. Among the
nine churches involved in the Consultation on Church Union
there have been varieties of doctrine on the Lord's Supper, or
Eucharist, or Holy Communion, and along with doctrinal differences there have been differences of Eucharistic practice.
Episcopalians and Disciples emphasize frequent Communion;
others celebrate monthly or quarterly. In some churches the
use of fermented wine is required; in others, unfermented
grape juice is the norm. In one, the only acceptable celebrant
is a priest ordained by a bishop. In another, the minister
preaches, but the prayer of consecration is said by lay elders.

While *Principles of Church Union* has not offered answers
to all these problems, the section of Chapter 3 on "The Lord's
Supper" is a remarkable example of the trend toward doctrinal
convergence among divided churches. To read it over before
going to Holy Communion would be a worthwhile exercise for
a member of any church as a way of enriching his understanding of the meaning of the sacrament.

In Roman Catholic circles, there is also a movement toward convergence on the subject of Eucharistic doctrine. The controversies of the Reformation seemed to lead to exaggerated positions on both sides: one proclaiming that the Mass was a genuine sacrifice and the other proclaiming that it was not, but with both sides lacking an adequate concept of what a sacrifice is. On the question of Christ's presence in the Eucharistic elements, again, both sides were attempting to express their position in philosophical terms which are no longer taken for granted: the concept of the "substance" or metaphysical reality of a thing, in distinction from its "accidents" or characteristics perceptible to the senses.

The Second Vatican Council, in the Constitution on the Church, says of the Holy Communion (Sec. 11): "Taking part in the eucharistic sacrifice, which is the fount and apex of the whole Christian life, they [the people of God] offer the divine victim to God and offer themselves along with it. Thus both by reason of the offering and through Holy Communion all take part in this liturgical service, not indeed all in the same way, but each in that way which is proper to himself. Strengthened in Holy Communion by the Body of Christ, they then manifest in a concrete way that unity of the People of God which is suitably symbolized and wondrously brought about by this most august sacrament."

This language would be unfamiliar to many of the participants in the Consultation on Church Union. But the sacrifice which is spoken of here is not thought of as an addition to the one sacrifice of Christ, nor as a repetition in some way of his sacrificial death but, rather, as an entering into and re-presentation of his one self-offering for the sins of the whole world.

A Joint Anglican-Roman Catholic Commission in the United States studied contemporary doctrinal statements of the two churches, particularly of the Vatican Council and the

Lambeth Conference of Anglican Bishops, and reported in May, 1967, that "it is clear to us that the findings of modern biblical, theological, and liturgical studies have transcended many of the polemical formulations of an earlier period." They summed up their consensus on the concept of Eucharistic sacrifice as follows:

The Church is the Body of Christ and is built up by the Word through the Eucharist.

Baptism is the entrance into the eucharistic community. In the Holy Eucharist Christians are united with Christ as the fulfillment and perfection of their baptismal union with him.

In the Lord's Supper we participate at the same time in Christ's death, resurrection, and ascension; the Christian community is thus transformed in grace and the pledge of future glory is given to us.

Our communion with Christ in the Holy Eucharist is also communion with one another. Such union is achieved through the Holy Spirit.

Christian people participating in Christ's priesthood through baptism and confirmation are meant to be a living sacrifice to God. That sacrifice finds its fullest expression in the eucharistic offering of the priesthood of the people of God. Such sacramental offering of the whole people is made possible through the special action of the ministerial priest, who is empowered by his ordination to make present Christ's sacrifice for his people.

The sacrifice of the Holy Eucharist is not just the sacrifice of the cross but the sacrifice of Christ's whole life of obedience to the Father which culminated in his death on the cross and his glorious resurrection. We offer nothing we have not first received; because of our incorporation into Christ at baptism, he offers us in himself to the Father.

The same basic idea of what happens in the Eucharist is expressed in *Principles of Church Union:* "The past is remembered, recalled as past events, but also remembered by way of being re-presented in the present as now operative and powerful. Holy Communion is an action of present communion undertaken in the confidence that through the Spirit Jesus Christ unites the members of the community of faith to himself and to each other. . . ." And, in the next paragraph, ". . . the action of the Church becomes the effective means whereby God in Christ acts and Christ is present with his people."

The Vatican Constitution on the Liturgy reminds us that the presence of Christ cannot be confined to one particular aspect of the service (Sec. 7):

To accomplish so great a work Christ is always present in His Church, especially in her liturgical celebrations. He is present in the sacrifice of the Mass, not only in the person of His minister, "the same now offering, through the ministry of priests, who formerly offered himself on the cross," but especially under the Eucharistic species. By His power He is present in the sacraments, so that when a man baptizes it is really Christ Himself who baptizes. He is present in His word, since it is He Himself who speaks when the holy scriptures are read in the Church. He is present, lastly, when the Church prays and sings, for He promised: "Where two or three are gathered together in my name, there am I in the midst of them."

Both Roman Catholics and Protestants have been restudying the teachings of Luther and Calvin on the Eucharistic sacrifice and Christ's presence in the sacrament. In the *Journal of Ecumenical Studies* (Vol. 2, No. 2), Roman Catholic James F. McCue points out that Luther had a doctrine of the Mass as a genuine sacrifice, quoting Luther's *Treatise on the New Testament, that is, the Holy Mass,* as follows:

To be sure, this sacrifice of prayer, praise, and thanksgiving and of ourselves as well, we are not to present before God in our own person. But we are to lay it upon Christ and let him present it for us as St. Paul teaches in Hebrews 13 [:15], "Let us continually offer up a sacrifice of praise to God, that is, the fruit of lips that confess him and praise him"; and all this "through Christ." For this is why he is also a priest—as Psalm 110 [:4] says, "You are a priest forever after the order of Melchizedek"—because he intercedes for us in heaven. He receives our prayer and sacrifice to God. Again St. Paul says in Hebrews 9 [:24], "He has ascended into heaven to be a mediator in the presence of God on our behalf," and in Romans 8 [:34], "It is Christ Jesus, who died, yes, who was raised from the dead, who sits on the right hand of God, who also makes intercession for us."

From these words we learn that we do not offer Christ as a sacrifice, but that Christ offers us. And in this way it is permissible, yes profitable, to call the Mass a sacrifice; not on its own account, but because we offer ourselves as a sacrifice along with Christ. . . . Christ takes up our cause, presents us and our prayer and praise, and also offers himself for us in heaven.

Dr. McCue asserts that "in substance Luther was actually holding the Roman Catholic position," but that he had good reason for attacking Roman Catholic practice, which treated the Mass as primarily "something to be used, a means to an end. Men want things from God and the Mass is *the* means of obtaining them. The Mass is an offering (a sacrifice) which, if correctly performed by the priest, influences God automatically (*ex opere operato*)."

This, Dr. McCue says, is a caricature of the Roman Catholic theological understanding of the Mass, but it was not created by Luther or the other Reformers. "It is a caricature that developed within Roman Catholicism and which to some extent is still to be found there." He rejoices that the liturgical movement has taken seriously the responsibility of making practice express doctrine within Roman Catholicism, and notes that practically all the changes made in recent liturgical reforms have been in the direction called for by Luther.

The author has a shrewd comment on the manner of doctrinal debate in the sixteenth century: "In an age in which Luther could say to Zwingli, 'Listen now, you pig, dog, or fanatic, whatever kind of unreasonable ass you are,' and Zwingli could reply by calling Luther a 'fanatic, fool, bumpkin, yes a devil, murderer, and corrupter of souls,' we must reckon with the *possibility* that adversaries would not listen to each other's refinements, clarifications, and extenuations with quite the openness which the seriousness of the subject would seem to require."

It is clear that, at the scholarly level at least, the movement toward convergence on the meaning of the Eucharist is far advanced. The chapter on the sacraments in *Principles of Church Union* is a significant part of this movement, representing not merely the drawing together of the nine churches in the Consultation but their part in a much wider movement engaging Roman Catholics, Lutherans, and the generality of the people of God.

As Professor John Dillenberger, of the United Church of Christ, observed in a paper given at the first meeting of the Consultation on Church Union (Washington, 1962): "From the Reformation into the 19th century, churches came into being out of an earnest concern for theological integrity and cultural relevance. Today, the same regard for theological integrity and meaningful witness demands the union of the churches. . . . The theological and cultural scene make mockery of our positions and disclose all too clearly that we are the victims of elusive and inertial factors which make it hard for us to die in order to live."

On the reality of Christ's presence in the sacrament, Calvin said: ". . . unless anyone would call God a deceiver, he can never presume to affirm that he sets before us an empty sign. Therefore, if by the breaking of the bread, the Lord really represents the participation of his body, it ought not to be doubted that he truly presents and communicates it, and it must always be a rule with believers whenever they see the signs instituted by the Lord, to assure and persuade themselves that they are also accompanied with the truth of the things signified. The visible sign is given to us to seal the donation of the invisible substance" (*Institutes,* cap. 17).

Accordingly, we can agree with the Vatican Council, in the passage previously quoted, that there is a special presence of Christ "under the Eucharistic species," but that he is present in the service in other ways as well: in the Church in general; in the person of his representative, the minister; in the sacramental action, in which it is really Christ who is acting; in his word; and in the prayers and praise of his people.

The Theological Commission of the United Church of Christ, in a response to *Principles of Church Union,* makes this significant affirmation (in words partly borrowed from a speech of a German bishop, Eduard Schick, at the Vatican Council):

The local church is the place where people listen together for the word of God and together enjoy the sacraments. It is not merely an administrative division of that great Church: it is a true representation and manifestation of the Church universal in which Christ, as the head of the Church, wholly lives and gives life. Even the total Church does not possess him in greater measure, for the whole Church is completely in its every part. This is an emphasis which the Eastern Orthodox Churches have never failed to make— "at the little gathering of priest and people about the altar of Christ in the remotest valley of Montenegro the entire Church, with all its saints and martyrs, is present"—and we believe that you [the Consultation on Church Union] are ready to make the same emphasis to no less a degree.

The U.C.C. Commission goes on to make the point that a

functional group for mission or service cannot be the Church unless it includes "week-after-week worship at a local altar, where one stands on the threshold between the eternal truths of Christ and the concrete needs of the group at worship, where minds are slowly contoured to the mind of Christ."

Several of the churches in the Consultation, together with some that are not members—notably the Roman Catholics and the Lutherans—are revising their orders for the service of Holy Communion in ways designed to express the growing convergence on principles of Christian worship which was discussed previously (see Chapter IV). One of the great themes of this movement is enhanced participation of the laity in the service—in prayers and responses and hymns, in bringing up the bread and wine, in reading the lessons. Another is the use of contemporary English. Another is more frequent celebration of the service among churches which have done so infrequently in the past and more frequent reception of Communion in churches where noncommunicating attendance has been widespread.

An Order of Service for the Lord's Supper, prepared by the Commission on Worship of the Consultation on Church Union and recommended to the churches, was used for the first time at the Consultation's 1968 meeting in Dayton, Ohio. Embodying contemporary liturgical understandings, it has aroused considerable interest among church people, and the Executive Committee of the Consultation has authorized its publication, by Forward Movement Publications, Cincinnati, Ohio, in 1968.

Thus a pattern of similarity in Eucharistic practice is developing which should be a most important resource for helping Christians to rediscover their unity in this, the sacrament of unity, as "Christ, the living Bread, gives himself to us, sustaining us and uniting us with himself and to each other."

Almighty and everliving God, we heartily thank you for feeding us with the spiritual food of the precious body and blood of your Son our Saviour Jesus Christ; and for assuring us thereby of your favor and goodness toward us; and for making us true members of the mystical body of your Son and heirs through hope of your everlasting kingdom. And we humbly ask you, heavenly Father, so to assist us by your Holy Spirit that we may continue in that holy fellowship and do all the tasks to which you have called us; through Jesus Christ our Lord, to whom with you and the Holy Spirit be all honor and glory, through endless ages. Amen.

VII

"Ministry...Accepted by All"

All of God's people in each place, according to the New Delhi statement on church unity, should not only be united among themselves in that place, but also "united with the whole Christian fellowship in all places and all ages in such wise that *ministry and members are accepted by all* and that all can act and speak together as occasion requires for the tasks to which God calls his people."

The churches involved in the Consultation on Church Union represent four distinct types of ministry. Four of them are Methodist bodies with bishops who are not regarded as belonging to a separate order of the ministry but as holding an office within the one ministry. However, this office is given great authority and responsibility in order to carry out the Methodist principle that every congregation has a right to a minister to preach the Word and administer the sacraments and that every minister has the right to a place to exercise his ministry.

The two Presbyterian churches hold strongly to the principle of the parity of the ministry; for them there is only one order of ministers, and episcopacy is exercised by the presbytery corporately, consisting of "teaching elders" (ministers) and an approximately equal number of "ruling elders" (lay persons set apart for their office of representing the laity in church government).

The United Church of Christ represents a union of two types of ministerial traditions—the Congregational and, from the Evangelical and Reformed Church, a ministry similar to the Presbyterian.

The Disciples of Christ represent a congregationalist position which gives a very prominent place to the laity in both worship and church government and guards the independence of the local congregation.

Only one of the nine, the Episcopal Church, seeks to maintain the three ancient orders of bishops, priests, and deacons, which were formerly characteristic of the entire Christian Church and remain the ministry of a substantial majority of present-day Christians, including the Eastern Orthodox and the Roman Catholics.

Partly to meet the need for responsible relation to the whole Christian fellowship both "in all places" and "in all ages," the Consultation on Church Union in its chapter on "The Ministry of the Church" recommends that a ministry of this general type, commonly called the "historic episcopate," be the ministry of the united Church. "Because this office is a principal symbol and means of continuity and unity of the Church, we therefore provide that bishops shall be chosen, consecrated, and governed in their ministry by the constitution of the united church," says the chapter on "The Ministry of the Church."

Similarly, provision is made for presbyters and deacons with the same general functions traditionally assigned to these offices in Christian history. The tasks of the bishop are defined as pastoral oversight (including guardianship of the faith), liturgical leadership, and administrative responsibility. As in the present-day life of the Episcopal Church, the bishop will function within a constitutional framework which gives both ministers and laymen a share of authority and responsibility in the Church's corporate decisions.

This measure of agreement, however, exists alongside sharp and deep-going differences of theory about the ministry. For example, the word "priest," although it is derived from the word "presbyter," has different connotations. It emphasizes the existence of special functions within the life of the Church which only an ordained person can perform, particularly the celebration of the Holy Communion. In classical theology, the priest must be ordained by a bishop standing in a line of succession that is believed to derive from the Apostles who were placed in the Church as its authoritative leadership by the Lord himself. *Principles of Church Union,* using the expression "presbyters (elders)" makes one reference to "the single priesthood which embraces every form of the presbyterate," but it specifically disavows "any one theory or doctrine" of either episcopate or presbyterate, asserting that no one doctrine on the subject has ever prevailed in the Church.

This assertion is in fact true. Popes have, on a few occasions, given a presbyter the authority to ordain men to the priesthood without consecrating him as a bishop. The Council of Trent, which launched post-Reformation Roman Catholicism, described the three "holy orders" as the orders of priest, deacon, and subdeacon, regarding the bishop as possessing "the fullness of the priesthood." There has long been uncertainty about which of the words of the ordination service are the essential "form" and what action constitutes the essential "matter" in ordination. Many other aspects of Catholic doctrine on the ministry are not as completely settled as is commonly believed.

Yet all these differences exist within the context of a ministry which is regarded as apostolic in origin and as *the* ministry which Christ intends his Church to have.

In churches of Reformation origin the problem is seen in a very different way. The grave abuses of ministerial power and authority against which the Reformers protested led them to the conclusion that the episcopate had forfeited any claim it might have to be apostolic. In the New Testament itself, the terms "bishop" and "presbyter" are used interchangeably (compare Acts 20:17 and 20:28 where "elders" equals "presbyters," and "guardians" is the word translated in other passages as "bishops"). Accordingly, appealing to the Scriptures against corruptions in the Church, some of the Reformers concluded that the pure and primitive state of the Church was one in which all presbyters and bishops were equal. If the Apostolate could be said to have continued at all, it did so in the persons of the presbyters.

Yet another theory of the ministry regards the general body of the Church as the source of Christian authority and the appointment of ministers as a practical arrangement—the minister is simply one of the laity appointed to a particular job.

The Consultation on Church Union has not been able to choose among these different basic theories or to find a promising line of convergence comparable to its statements on Scripture and Tradition, on baptism, and on Holy Communion. Dr. Grayston's remarks on spirituality and church order, quoted in Chapter IV, are also relevant here. These things are our several ways of being Christian, and they cannot be discarded or modified at will. He went on to say:

My second term was *church order,* which was intended to indicate the means by which the will of God for his people is discovered and put into operation. It is the cohesiveness of a Christian community, the network of personal relationships which makes a living church possible. I do not refer simply to the hierarchy of a church (which can be as evident among Protestant Christians as among Catholics) nor to the official committees and consultative bodies, but the total structure by which real decisions as distinct from official pronouncements become effective within the church and by which the real energies of the church are engaged in this rather than in that direction. . . . By church order I mean, as it were, the muscular structure and nervous system of the Body of Christ which makes possible the church's participation in (or possibly withdrawal from) the life of the world.

While doctrines of the ministry are not the only constituent element in church order (and, indeed, conflicting doctrines exist within the fellowship of each church), in church union discussions the different types of relations among ministers and between ministers and members serve to symbolize this vital area of church life: the ethos, the way of living and working together under God which seems to belong to a divinely sanctioned order of things.

Every church believes that the Holy Spirit works within it, guiding it and empowering it in its worship, witness, and service. Thus church order has a theological dimension, whether the bishop, or the presbyteries, or the congregations be thought of as the principal body through which the Spirit guides the Church to a deeper understanding of the scriptural revelation and its demands for contemporary living. It is not easy to compromise on an issue such as this.

Thoughtful scholarly comments from responsible groups in churches participating in the Consultation make diametrically opposite recommendations about the chapter on the ministry. The Theological Commission of the United Church of Christ says: "When we read . . . 'the historic episcopate commends itself as personifying the continuity of churchly authority,' we detect the faintest breath of what to us (and, we believe, to most of the Church) is a bygone theory—the theory that churchly authority exists primarily in the episcopal office, whose incumbents are therefore in a position to personify it in the dimension of continuity."

This bygone theory was stoutly supported, however, in a comment from the Episcopal diocese of Spokane, which found the Consultation's position lacking by the yardstick of the Episcopal Church's Statement of Faith and Order of 1949: "The Church is set before us in the New Testament as a body of believers having within it, as its recognized focus of unity, of teaching, and of authority, the Apostolate, which owed its origin to the action of the Lord himself."

From the Presbyterian Dubuque Theological Seminary came a comment that rode off in several directions at once: "*(a)* Bishops as representations of the unity of the Church, that is, emphasis on the historic episcopate, were rejected. *(b)* Bishops as functioning for needed administrative tasks were accepted. *(c)* Bishops as central to the full understanding of the unity of the Church, and from which all clerical functions flow, were advocated." To which the Dubuque report adds: "Obviously, faculty members were divided on this one!"

Some of the boldest and most creative thinking about the doctrine of the ministry is going on among Roman Catholic theologians. The Second Vatican Council, while strongly re-affirming long-established dogmatic positions, opened up several doors to theological development.

First is the concept of the Church as the "people of God," possessing the "dignity and freedom of the Sons of God, in whose hearts the Holy Spirit dwells as in his temple. Its law is the new commandment to love as Christ loved us. Its end is the kingdom of God, which has been begun by God himself on earth, and which is to be further extended until it is brought to perfection by him at the end of time" (Constitution on the

Church, Sec. 9). The faithful share in Christ's priesthood (Sec. 11) and in his prophetic office (Sec. 12). Christians who do not belong to the Roman Catholic Church still share in important ways in the common life of the people of God (Sec. 15). Even those who have not yet received the gospel are "related in various ways to the People of God" (Sec. 16).

This clear-cut distinction between the Church in pilgrimage and the perfected kingdom of God as the end of the pilgrimage has become a powerfully liberating force in almost every aspect of Roman Catholic thought.

Second is the doctrine of the collegiality of bishops. They are not mere assistants of the Pope, but a body appointed by Christ, under the presidency of the Pope, to rule and guide and feed the Church. In the same spirit, the bishops are to share their responsibilities with the priests, and the priests with the people. Relevant passages from the Constitution on the Church are:

[Sec. 18]: This sacred Council, following closely in the footsteps of the First Vatican Council, with that Council teaches and declares that Jesus Christ, the eternal Shepherd, established his holy Church, having sent forth the apostles as he himself had been sent by the Father (cf. Jn 20, 21); he willed that their successors, namely the bishops, should be shepherds in his Church even to the consummation of the world. And in order that the episcopate itself might be one and undivided, he placed blessed Peter over the other apostles, and instituted in him a permanent and visible source and foundation of unity of faith and communion. And this teaching about the institution, the perpetuity, the meaning and reason for the sacred primacy of the Roman pontiff and of his infallible magisterium, this sacred Council again proposes to be firmly believed by all the faithful. . . .

[Sec. 20]: Bishops, therefore, with their helpers, the priests and deacons, have taken up the service of the community, presiding in place of God over the flock, whose shepherds they are, as teachers for doctrine, priests for sacred worship, and ministers for government. And just as the office granted individually to Peter, the first among the apostles, is permanent and is to be transmitted to his successors, so also the apostles' office of nurturing the Church is to be exercised without interruption by the sacred order of bishops. Therefore, the sacred Council teaches that bishops, by divine institution, have succeeded to the place of the apostles as shepherds of the Church, and he who hears them hears Christ, and he who rejects them rejects Christ and him who sent Christ (cf. Luke 10, 16).

And the third door that the Council opened was the door to dialogue with other Christians and deeper respect for their "Churches and ecclesial communities," as briefly indicated in the Constitution on the Church and spelled out more fully in the Decree on Ecumenism.

Within this broader area of operations, Roman Catholic scholars have been searching for common ground with Protestants on the meaning of sacraments and ministry. In an article in the *Journal of Ecumenical Studies* (Winter, 1966), Father Frans Jozef van Beek, director of studies of the Dutch Jesuit Province, sketches the changed state of the question:

Ever since the Catholic Church has become more consciously aware of its own pilgrim state, not excluding the level of unity as willed and promised by Christ, since it has recognized that it is also on its way to "the unity of the faith and of the knowledge of the Son of God, to mature manhood, to the measure of the stature of the fullness of Christ" (Ephesians 4:13), it has also become more alive to the good faith of other Christian communities, which —like itself, and, in the World Council of Churches, more effectively for the time being—are also on their way to unity. The essential unity of the Church is no longer merely conceived as a circumscriptive, juridically outlined, fixed unity of order; it has also, and preeminently, come to be viewed as Christ's eschatological gift to his perfect community. It is for this unity that the Churches have to prepare themselves by a growth toward vital, not necessarily uniform, unity among themselves.

On this principle, Father van Beek sees possibilities for ultimate recognition by the Roman Catholic Church of non-Catholic formulations of doctrine and sacraments and ministry as, like its own, "capable only of truly realizing salvation in an incomplete manner. A church conscious of its pilgrim state will *in concreto* always realize that these limitations of its creed and church order make it at least possible for the Kingdom to be concretized along different lines and that *de facto* other churches exist by its side."

In the Winter issue of the same journal a year later, the veteran ecumenist George Tavard arrives at some significant conclusions:

I have made a distinction between the minister acting as *elder* or trusted delegate of the community, and the minister acting as sacramental person, set apart by the community or its representatives in order to receive sacramental ordination. In the first capacity, he is *presbyter,* in the etymological sense of the word; in the second he is *priest,* in the traditional meaning of this term. Catholic thought has accented the priestly character of the minister, at the same time paying little attention to the minister as elder among the people, whereas Protestant thought is, by and large, agreed on the minister as elder, but not on his function as priest. From the standpoint of Catholic thought, there should be no difficulty in acknowledging the ministers of Protestant Churches to be elders in their communities, and thus recognizing that, despite the lack of a doctrine of sacramental orders, they have eccelesiological status beyond that of baptized laymen.

This degree of recognition, however, is not enough. The Protestant must insist that his ministry is in every sense as complete a ministry of Christ as that of the Catholic priest. If he is an elder only, so is the priest who thinks himself to be something more. If the priest is something more than an elder, so is the minister. But Father Tavard continues:

One more step may be tentatively envisaged. . . . The reality of the laying on of hands according to apostolic practice implies an intentionality of its own which is no more fully negated by theological denials than it is expressed by theological endorsements. Life in the body of the Church is richer than its doctrinal expression. We may therefore wonder if, where the intention has remained to provide for the continuity of the preaching of the Gospel according to Christ's design, the reality of the sacrament has not passed into the laying on of hands practiced in the Churches issuing from the Reformation, albeit outside normal episcopal channels and despite Protestant sacramental doctrines or the lack of them.

In the dialogue of the Roman Catholic Church in America with the Presbyterian and other Reformed churches, significant work is being done to think through the implications of the new ecumenical situation for doctrines of the ministry. It is possible that this group, although at present its findings are highly tentative, will bring about the needed breakthrough to arrive at a genuine consensus (see Appendix, p. 185).

Once basic agreement is arrived at on what the ministry of the united Church is and does, the problem remains of unifying the ministry, of assuring that every minister can be accepted in good conscience by every congregation as a properly ordained minister of Christ.

In the Church of South India, so far the only united Church that has come into being that included both episcopal and nonepiscopal ministers, the rule was made that all future ministers would be ordained by bishops, but that those who had already been ordained would simply be accepted without regard to the kind of ordination they had received. There was a proviso that no congregation would be required to accept a minister against its conscientious scruples over a thirty-year period from the inauguration of the union in 1947. Most of the Anglican provinces, including the Episcopal Church in the U.S.A., adopted a policy of granting full recognition to former Anglican presbyters and to presbyters ordained by a bishop in the Church of South India itself, but not to those who had not been episcopally ordained. This made for an unhappy situation all around.

In an attempt to solve this problem, most union plans since that time have included a "service of unification" so designed that it would clearly affirm the reality and efficacy of all the ministries of the uniting churches. It also included a prayer for whatever each might need of God's grace, authority, and power for his future ministry, together with the laying on of the bishop's hands. It is recognized that different people will have different ideas about the significance of such an action, but it is intended to clear up any doubts in anyone's mind about the full spiritual equality of all.

Principles of Church Union indicates an intention to pursue some such course in its reference to "a corporate act in which and through which all would offer our existing ministries to Almighty God, asking him to receive our offerings through Jesus Christ, to complete and perfect what is amiss or incomplete in our ministries, and to give us whatever of his authority and grace we need to serve in the united ministry to which we are called."

This approach has both good points and bad ones. It requires a large measure of Christian charity for a minister who has no doubt whatever of the reality of his ordination to defer to the scruples of those who do have doubts. But such a selfless identification with the needs of erring humanity has its scriptural model in the willingness of Jesus to be baptized by John the Baptist.

Almighty God, our heavenly Father, mercifully look upon the universal Church which you have purchased at the cost of the precious blood of your dear Son, and so guide and govern the minds of your servants, the Bishops and Pastors of your flock that they lay hands suddenly on no man, but faithfully and wisely choose fit persons to serve in the sacred ministry. And to those who are ordained to any holy function give your grace and heavenly blessing, that both by their life and teaching they may show forth your glory and set forward the salvation of all men; through Jesus Christ our Lord. Amen.

VIII

The Ministry of the Members

In *Principles of Church Union,* the section on the ministry rightly begins with the ministry of the laity—the prophetic, priestly, and royal character of the Church as a whole, and of every member individually. "Our ministry to one another in the community of Christians and our ministry as individuals and as the whole people of God in and for the world is therefore one ministry, the ministry of Christ."

However, there is something to be said for reversing the logical order to dispose of the rough part of the subject first and then sail into smoother waters. For the ministry of the laity is another subject on which the vast movement of theological convergence has brought Christians of many different traditions into substantial agreement.

The process of liturgical reform in all the churches is closely connected with the new understanding of the layman as a full-fledged Christian in whom Christ dwells and to whom and in whom the Spirit speaks, as a man who has direct access in Christ to God the Father. The theological basis for this understanding is, of course, biblical. It is the theme of the whole First Epistle of Peter, especially the famous passage, "But you are a chosen race, a royal priesthood, a holy nation, God's own people, that you may declare the wonderful deeds of him who called you out of darkness into his marvelous light" (I Peter 2:9). And it was one of the great contributions of the sixteenth-century Reformation to a recovery of biblical understandings.

This recovery was spurred in part by the struggle to defend the laity from excessive claims of the clergy to be the means of human approach to God, and, as commonly happens in controversy, there was a tendency to exaggeration on both sides. The ideal situation for relations among the various orders in the Church is that of the Council of Jerusalem (Acts 15), where "the apostles and the elders, with the whole Church" came to a common mind. But even among the Churches of the Reformation, there has been a tendency to regard the clergy as full-time Christians and the laity as part-time Christians, and to use the word "church," not for the people of the Church, as in the Book of Acts, but for its officers.

At the Bossey Consultation on Church Union Negotiations, a report was given by William Stewart of the (Presbyterian) Church of Scotland on "Church Union and the Ministry of the Laity," pointing out the development from the South India scheme of 1947, which confined its view of lay ministry almost entirely to in-church ministries, to the current understanding of the whole Church and all its members as being equally engaged in Christ's priestly ministry of worship of the Father and service to the world.

One of the best statements of this ministry is found in the proposed basis of union of the Anglican, Presbyterian, and Methodist Churches in Ghana, Africa. It reads:

The negotiating Churches recognize that it is the duty and privilege of every member to share in that service of God which is the ministry of the whole Church. This ministry includes the worship of God both in private and in public, the offering of daily life and work to God, Christian loving service both in the family of the Church and in the community at large, and faithful witness to the Gospel of Jesus Christ by life and word. Within this ministry the negotiating Churches recognize and welcome a rich diversity of gifts both in men and in women. It will be a prime concern of the united Church that all its members should contribute fully to its life of worship, witness, and service.

Lay people are called to witness and serve primarily in their daily work and in the life of the community, and not only within the institutional life of the Church. Lay people are the Church in daily ministry to the world, witnessing, serving, and praying within each human situation. The united Church must provide ways by which lay people can be equipped for and supported in this difficult ministry in the world.

Only after this does the document turn to the ministries within the Church of lay professionals and volunteers and such specially commissioned lay ministries as elders, local preachers, and catechists in charge of congregations. The section then concludes, in language largely drawn from the South India union scheme:

Members of the Church should constantly bear in mind that their different forms of ministry both to those within the Church and to those outside it, are only of value for the carrying out of God's purposes in so far as the Holy Spirit is working through those ministries in the hearts of men. The ministry of intercession, therefore, is vital and it should not only underlie and inspire all those forms of ministry outlined in this section, but be recognized as one which should constantly be exercised by all members of the Church. Those who are debarred by sickness or other causes from exercising other ministries should recognize their call to the duty and privilege of this ministry of intercession.

Principles of Church Union presents essentially the same view of the role of the laity in Church life at the beginning of Chapter 4, winding up with this statement: "Our ministry to one another in the community of Christians and our ministry as individuals and as the whole people of God in and for the world is therefore one ministry, the ministry of Christ.

No differences of vocation or ordination should obscure the fact that our ministry is one and that it is so only by reason of its participation in Christ's ministry, which is the ministry of the Father through the Incarnate Son by the Spirit. An incarnate Word demands a gospel incarnated in the daily lives of the people of God."

Here again, significant parallels can be found in the actions of the Vatican Council, in a radical upgrading of the laity in almost every aspect of that Church's life.

The theological basis for this change was set forth in the Constitution on the Church with its emphasis on the biblical image of the Church as the people of God. In Chapter IV, "The Laity," it is asserted that the clergy "were not ordained by Christ to take upon themselves the entire salvific mission of the Church toward the world." The laity, no less than the clergy are "by baptism made one body with Christ and are constituted among the people of God. They are in their own way made sharers in the priestly, prophetical, and kingly functions of Christ and they carry out for their own part the mission of the whole Christian people in the Church and in the world."

Other important points mentioned in the Constitution are: "The Laity," it is asserted that the clergy "were not ordained press their opinion on those things which concern the good of the Church." They should "accept in Christian obedience the decisions of their pastors," but there is new advice for pastors: "Let pastors recognize and promote the dignity as well as the responsibility of the laity in the Church. Let them willingly employ their prudent advice. Let them confidently assign duties to them in the service of the Church, allowing them freedom and room for action. Further, let pastors encourage lay people so that they may undertake tasks on their own initiative."

These sweeping affirmations of the dignity and freedom of

the laity are reflected in the Council's Decree on the Apostolate of the Laity, which passed by the overwhelming vote of 2,208 affirmative, 2 negative, 5 void. Interpreting Ephesians 4:16, the Decree asserts: "The Christian vocation by its very nature is also a vocation to the apostolate. No part of the structure of a living body is merely passive but has a share in the functions as well as the life of the body. . . . In the Church there is a diversity of ministry but a oneness of mission.

"The laity exercise their apostolate in fact by their activity directed to the evangelization and sanctification of men and to the penetrating and perfecting of the temporal order through the spirit of the Gospel."

Much of the Decree is devoted to practical applications of these principles in church, personal, family, and social life. Both in the U.S.A. and in various European countries many steps have been taken since the Council, to carry out these concepts. Bishops hold periodic meetings with both clergy and laity to discuss and discover problems and to consider proposed solutions. Laymen have been elevated to positions of authority in school boards and other church institutions such as seminary boards, diocesan papers, and welfare bureaus. In several dioceses the laity are provided representation in the diocesan synod.

Diocesan synods themselves, although provided for in canon law, had virtually gone out of existence until Pope John XXIII, who called for a meeting of the synod of his own diocese of Rome at the same time that he called for a council of the whole Church. Now they are being called for in many dioceses around the world.

Such internal developments in Roman Catholic life are perhaps even more important ecumenically than the improved relations between Rome and the other Christian churches. They represent the growing up of a common Christian life, a mutuality in Christian fellowship, which must develop if ecclesiastical unity is ever to be achieved. For while the Church has thrived in many different types of society, it is inconceivable in today's world that those who experience Christian freedom and dignity in their own church life could return to the authoritarian patterns of the past.

All the churches in the Consultation provide for substantial representation of the laity at all levels of church government. The Disciples of Christ still retain vestiges of the New England town meeting in their polity; any member of that church may come to the General Assembly and is entitled to all privileges except voting; this, under a recent restructure, will be reserved to ministers and lay representatives from each congregation, plus a few others by virtue of their office.

Among the other churches, a more republican type of structure exists with full representation of clergy and laity. The Episcopal Church provides additional checks and balances by dividing its General Convention into two houses: a House of Bishops and a House of Deputies. The presbyters and laymen of the latter house vote separately on controversial matters, and no measure can pass that is not approved by a majority in each order.

A sketch of the structure of the united Church is not yet in existence, except for a proposed provisional assembly which will probably sit as one house and consist of clergy and laity in approximately equal numbers, with twenty-five or more representatives selected by each of the uniting churches.

At the 1968 meeting in Dayton, Ohio, where this proposal for a provisional assembly with an executive body called a provisional council was received and passed on to a working Commission for further development, a lively issue came up over the question of additional representatives for churches with more than a million members. Equality of representation was carried by a margin of one vote, on the plea of the three Negro denominations participating in the Consultation.

At present, the Episcopal Church is the only one that excludes women from its legislature, but a constitutional amendment has been passed on first reading to correct this archaic, if not obsolete, practice.

In spite of all these affirmations of the importance of the laity, there is discernible in the life of American Christianity an odd and growing estrangement between many of the laity and a substantial section of the clergy. Perhaps the difficulty is that the laity do not seem to be making much of an effort to fulfill the vocation that is so glowingly described for them; perhaps in the pressing issues of our time—in race relations, in the problems of the use of America's military power, in the responsibilities of wealthy nations to underdeveloped nations —the clergy feel that the laity are not responding strongly enough to what they believe to be the demands of Christian concern for mankind.

A recent cartoon in *The New Yorker* pointed up the subject. The congregation leaving a fashionable church was shown fighting and quarreling among themselves, as the rector swung his fist at an elderly critic. The caption was: "Goodness, what do you suppose the rector's message for the troubled world was this time?"

And this leads logically into the next task for tomorrow's Church: the task of renewal.

> *Direct us, O Lord, in all our doings, with your gracious favour, and further us with your continual help; that in all our works begun, continued, and ended in you, we may glorify your holy Name, and finally, by your mercy, obtain everlasting life; through Jesus Christ our Lord. Amen.*

IX

"The Tasks to Which God Calls His People"

Throughout the Christian world today runs a seething movement of response to the extraordinary changes in the human condition that have taken place in recent years. The churches in the Consultation on Church Union are deeply involved in this movement, although in the nature of the case the Consultation is only one of their many instruments for reaching out "in witness and service to all" in local communities and acting and speaking together nationally and internationally for "the tasks to which God calls his people."

Some of the characteristics of the world in which God is acting today are well described in the Vatican Council's Constitution on the Church in the Modern World:

Today, the human race is involved in a new stage of history. Profound and rapid changes are spreading by degrees around the whole world. Triggered by the intelligence and creative energies of man, these changes recoil upon him, upon his decisions and desires, both individual and collective, and upon his manner of thinking and acting with respect to things and people. Hence we can already speak of a true cultural and social transformation, one which has repercussions upon man's religious life as well.

As happens in any crisis of growth, this transformation has brought serious difficulties in its wake. Thus while man extends his power in every direction, he does not always succeed in subjecting it to his own welfare. Striving to probe more profoundly into the deeper recesses of his own mind, he frequently appears more unsure of himself. Gradually and more precisely he lays bare the laws of society, only to be paralyzed by uncertainty about the direction to give it.

Never has the human race enjoyed such an abundance of wealth, resources, and economic power, and yet a huge proportion of the world's citizens are still tormented by hunger and poverty, while countless millions suffer from total illiteracy. Never before has man had so keen an understanding of freedom, yet at the same time, new forms of social and psychological slavery make their appearance. Although the world of today has a very vivid awareness of its unity and of how one man depends on another in needful solidarity, it is most grievously torn into opposing camps by conflicting forces. For political, social, economic, racial, and ideological disputes still continue bitterly, and with them the peril of a war which would reduce everything to ashes.

The new situation of mankind has had a profound impact on the Church's own self-understanding. New theologies, new concepts of Christian morality, new meanings for such basic Christian terms as "mission" and "evangelism" combine with new patterns of action and involvement, new forms of ministry, and new priorities for the churches' use of money and manpower, to produce what appears to be a radically altered relationship between the Church and the world.

History suggests that when the Church becomes action-oriented it does not always act wisely. The crusades of the Middle Ages and the prohibition experiment of the twentieth century are examples. Similarly, a theology which embraces secular society too uncritically may find itself supporting not only a more abundant life for man but demonic forces that tend toward new enslavement and hatred among men. A false eschatology—a mistaken belief in the ability of men to bring in the kingdom of God by their own efforts—drives well-intentioned Christians into extremes of thought and action which those who follow after them may have to repent, as the clergy later repented their uncritical militarism in World War I.

Nevertheless, it is true that twentieth-century man has radically new possibilities both for good and for evil, and that the Church cannot fail to concern itself with the new dimensions thus imposed upon the commandment to love one's neighbor as oneself.

In the chapter on "The Faith of the Church," the Consultation touches upon the continuing responsibility of the Church to represent its servant Lord in the world:

Inheriting the apostolic vocation the united Church is called to exercise its reconciling mission, both to individuals and to the power-structures of the world. Its efforts to fulfill this commission will therefore form a major mode of confessing its faith. It will seek continually to clarify its understanding of the eternal gospel, and to convey that understanding in its public appeal to the world. It will seek to translate the essentials of Christian faith into terms intelligible to men, without weakening the demands which are intrinsic to Christ's work as Judge and Redeemer of all. It will speak to the contemporary issues of public life, knowing the conflict between "the wisdom of God" and "the wisdom of this age," and knowing also that Christ has reconciled the world to God. Serving in Christ's name and example, the Church will translate its faith as it gives itself in suffering love for the world. Only in such translation of faith into deeds will the Church participate in the suffering and glory of the Crucified and Risen Lord. In each situation it will give its grateful witness to the presence of God, who rules and over-rules the affairs of men and nations.

The churches have been struggling, both severally and collectively, to carry out this mission in many vital areas of society—in race relations, in war and peace, especially the

Vietnam war, in the problems of poverty at home and under-development abroad. In each of these areas it seems that for the first time man has the physical means to choose between abundant living and unimaginable disaster for all. As to the people of Israel in the wilderness, God is saying to us today: "I call heaven and earth to witness against you this day, that I have set before you life and death, blessing and curse; therefore choose life, that you and your descendants may live, loving the LORD your God, obeying his voice, and cleaving to him . . ." (Deuteronomy 30:19-20).

In the World Council of Churches and the National Council of Churches, Christians work together to carry out this common mission. More and more, such efforts are coordinated with those of the Roman Catholic Church, particularly at local levels, and in many programs ways are found for common action with the Jewish community and secular groups as well.

Voluntary groups of Christians and other concerned persons, crossing denominational lines, go far beyond official Church positions on matters on which the churches themselves are divided—for example, openly urging young men to refuse military service. When clergy are prominent in these activities, using such tactics as sit-ins and protest marches, some laymen feel that the prestige of the Church is being unfairly identified with one side of a controversial issue. Radical theologians emphasize the secular, this-worldly dimension of Christianity, reminding us that God loves the world and therefore created the Church to serve it.

All these things, as noted in the preceding chapter, have an unsettling effect upon parish life. Just after telling the laity that they are a royal priesthood and ministers of Christ, the Church tells them that the whole character of their church life is in radical need of reform. Some of our prophets insist that the structure of the ordinary Christian congregation is hopelessly out of date, and it appears that a majority of present-day theological students wish to enter some other form of ministerial service. Among some of the radicals, the whole idea of church unity seems a waste of energy—the Church talking to itself instead of the world.

Meanwhile, in several of the churches in the Consultation, little groups of conservative church members have concluded that the Church is being perverted from its true mission and have withdrawn and formed congregations and denominations of their own. At the other end of the scale, among Roman Catholics, an "underground church" has sprung up, concelebrating the Holy Communion with Anglicans, Orthodox, and Protestants in private homes and taking counsel together on radical Christian obedience in this time and this place.

These are symptoms of the movement of Christian renewal, the impact of the "cultural and social transformation" on the life of the Church and the efforts of the Church to be obedient to God under new conditions of life. In a document adopted a year after *Principles of Church Union,* entitled *Guidelines for the Structure of the Church,* the Consultation noted that the former document was principally concerned with "the enduring structures of the Church—its faith, worship, sacraments, and ministry." These enduring structures of the Church "enable it to change in response to the necessities of and opportunities for mission in the world. It is not these, but the structures instrumental to the mission which are our present concern."

Two relevant paragraphs in this document are:

Structures providing for a corporate witness and ministry in the several communities in which men live are required in a united church. Such structures are not substitutes for the witness and ministry of the individual Christian. The encouragement and equipment of the individual Christian for witness and ministry is of central importance. But structures are also required so that the claims of justice and peace and love can be held before men and human societies. Structures are also required to discharge a corporate ministry in the communities of research and experiment, in communities of production and distribution of goods, in communities of organized social life, and in other communities in which men live and work.

Structures are required for sustaining and furthering the dialogue between the community of faith and these other communities; for participation as a partner in the enduring struggle to utilize natural resources, knowledge, technology and social organization, to make available enhanced opportunities for an increasing number of men to live a fuller human life; for participation in the struggle to resist the destructive and disintegrating forces which threaten man's life.

Thus the Consultation sees tomorrow's Church as taking with utmost seriousness the challenge of the times, but also as sturdily maintaining the one faith which has been articulated in many different cultural settings in the past. It is not worried about the "death of God." On the contrary, it is pricked into action by the goading of the living God who sets before men his demand that they choose for themselves between life and death.

The Rev. W. B. Blakemore, of the Disciples of Christ, in an article in the *Catholic World* for June, 1965, had a significant comment on the ferment in the life of the churches today:

One may feel that if there are so very many questions to answer, neither Catholics nor Protestants are any longer very sure of themselves. On the contrary, both those Catholics and those Protestants who are now asking themselves these questions are more sure of their faith than they have ever been. These are not questions that are being asked out of religious insecurity and confusion. They are questions that are being asked out of a renewed faith which looks at the existing realities and knows that there is room for improvement and development and recognizes that the way forward needs to be found. When men are spiritually insecure they do not ask such questions but fall back on rigid dogmatism. What has happened is that being launched into the ecumenical movement is an experience of an increase in the Christian virtues of faith, hope and love in such a way that without defensiveness all the lesser questions can be asked: the questions about authority, about Church organization, about adequate ways of stating the doctrine. These questions are asked without fear that while we are asking them our fundamental faith will be toppled over.

The necessity for rapid change brings its own dangers and disruptions. Tolstoy, in *War and Peace,* says that in Napoleon's retreat from Moscow the Russian army, pursuing, lost almost as many men as the fleeing army of the French, simply because both armies were traveling too fast. In church renewal, there will be quite a bit more Church on hand for renewing if the process is not carried on at excessive speed. The clergy naturally are the first to grasp the meaning of the cultural revolution for church life, and they should give the laity some time to catch up.

Yet against this worldly wisdom may be set Jesus' own urgency in his preaching of the kingdom: "Leave the dead to bury their own dead; but as for you, go and proclaim the kingdom of God. . . . No one who puts his hand to the plow and looks back is fit for the kingdom of God" (Luke 9:60, 62). In God's dealings with men, there is a time of visitation *(episkope),* a day of judgment, a moment when God says, "Now!" It is interesting that the word used in Christ's lament for Jerusalem (Luke 19:44) is from the same root as the Greek word for "bishop."

In *Second Living Room Dialogues,* designed for use by Roman Catholic, Orthodox, Anglican, and Protestant lay people in dialogue, the themes are those of church renewal. The chapter headings are: The Church in the World; To-

morrow's World; The Generation Gap; The North-South Di-
lemma (referring to have and have-not nations in the world
as a whole, rather than the U.S., North and South); The
Dignity of Man; War and Peace; The Person in the Modern
World (with special attention to the new morality); and The
Church, Charismatic and Institutional. Perhaps subjects such
as these are more basic to the life of tomorrow's Church and
its laity than the details of plans of church union. Not every-
one needs to be involved in problems of church government,
but every confirmed Christian needs to confront the issues of
Christian living in today's world.

This, indeed, is the concluding message of the Vatican
Constitution on the Church in the Modern World:

> Mindful of the Lord's saying, "by this will all men know that
> you are my disciples, if you have love for one another" (John
> 13:35), Christians cannot yearn for anything more ardently than
> to serve the men of the modern world ever more generously and
> effectively. Therefore, by holding faithfully to the Gospel and
> benefiting from its resources, Christians have shouldered a gigantic
> task to be carried out in this world, a task concerning which they
> must give a reckoning to Him who will judge every man on the
> last day.
>
> Not everyone who cries, "Lord, Lord," will enter the kingdom
> of heaven, but those who do the Father's will by taking a strong
> grip on the work at hand. Now, the Father wills that in all men
> we recognize Christ our brother and love him effectively in word
> and in deed. By thus giving witness to the truth, we will share
> with others the mystery of the heavenly Father's love. As a con-
> sequence, men throughout the world will be aroused to a lively
> hope—the gift of the Holy Spirit that finally they will be caught
> up in peace and utter happiness in that fatherland radiant with the
> glory of the Lord.

The golden text that sums up the whole gospel will still
possess its full power in tomorrow's Church: "For God so
loved the world that he gave his only Son, that whoever be-

lieves in him should not perish but have eternal life. For God sent the Son into the world, not to condemn the world, but that the world might be saved through him." For the gospel is indeed about everlasting life and a glorious consummation for redeemed humanity.

Principles of Church Union bears its witness to the Church's age-long faith in this destiny of mankind in many passages. In the chapter on "The Faith of the Church," it testifies to "the glorious consummation of his Kingdom which has no end" and sees each congregation as "the mysterious and marvelous work of God, intended by him for a destiny of ceaseless praise."

It sees baptism as giving a new life which "transcends mortal life and death. . . . a foretaste of the eternal life promised by Christ," a sign that God will raise us and all creation "out of nothingness into his new creation at the last day."

It sees the Holy Communion as "the presence of Christ who has come, who comes to his people, and who will come in glory. It is the anticipation and foretaste of the heavenly banquet where the redeemed people of God will eat and drink with their crucified and risen Lord in his kingdom."

But belief in this eternal gospel does not permit Christians to be unconcerned with the life of the world around them—indeed, as the New Testament never tires of reminding us, every deed of mercy, every act of justice done to the least of men is a service to humanity's Servant King. It is undoubtedly reasonable to suspect that some of the voices urging the Church to involvement in secular society come from thinkers whose perception of the spiritual dimension of life has dimmed, and we must pray that God will open their eyes; yet what they are telling us about God's demands on us in the secular city is utterly, scripturally true.

At every level of meaningful human existence—the family,

the neighborhood, the metropolitan area, the state, the nation, the world—the gospel demands to be proclaimed, the kingdom needs to be exhibited in action. And if this is true, then tomorrow's Church must be so organized that "all can act and speak together as occasion requires for the tasks to which God calls his people."

> *Almighty God, who created man in your own image: Grant us grace fearlessly to contend against evil and to make no peace with oppression; and, that we may reverently use our freedom, help us to employ it in the maintenance of justice among men and nations, to the glory of your holy Name; through Jesus Christ our Lord. Amen.*

X

"Brought by the Holy Spirit..."

Unity is made visible, the New Delhi statement says, as all who are baptized into Christ and confess him as Lord and Saviour "are brought by the Holy Spirit into one fully committed fellowship." The phrase calls to mind St. Paul's concluding words in II Corinthians: "The grace of the Lord Jesus Christ and the love of God and the *fellowship* of the Holy Spirit be with you all."

In their brief summaries of the main themes of the New Testament, the Apostles' and Nicene Creeds confess the Christian's faith in the Holy Spirit, and, as a corollary, faith in the holy Catholic Church. It is not fashionable in Protestant circles these days to look upon the Church as an object of faith, and in Roman Catholic circles, too, a keen awareness has grown up that the Church is in constant need of reform and renewal, of rededication to its divine origin and purpose.

A catalogue of the corporate sins of Christian people down the ages would make melancholy reading, beginning with that Thursday evening when the Lord's disciples all forsook him and fled at the moment of crisis, and going on through riots, crusades, pogroms, inquisitions, and wars, not to mention the racism of our own day. Some theological traditions attempt to

solve the problem of the divine and the human in the life of
the Church by dividing it into two realities—the visible
Church in which good and bad are entwined together and the
invisible Church, known only to God, in which the divine
reigns unchallenged and unstained. But, as Professor J. Robert
Nelson points out in his recent book, *Crisis in Unity and
Witness,* this is too easy a way of getting around the problem.
The Church that is written about in the New Testament is the
same Church whether it is being lauded as "the pillar and
bulwark of the truth" (I Timothy 3:15) or excoriated for mis-
behavior, false doctrine, and faithlessness, as in Paul's Cor-
inithian epistles and the letters to the seven churches in the
book of Revelation.

Dr. Nelson says:

It is strange that many Christians, who are faithful and active
members of the visible church in the place where they live, believe
only in this unhistorical, spiritualized invisible church. Others are
more consistent, however, and remain apart from the visible
church, which they disdain as a haven of hypocrites. But, if
people cannot believe on the basis of what they see that the
church is a particular work of God, they will not be convinced that
somewhere beyond the clouds or in the sweet by-and-by there is
an honest-to-God true church.

Thus, the distinction between the visible and invisible church
does not adequately explain the nature of the church. It does not
sufficiently reflect the Biblical understanding of the church, and it
does not satisfy the contemporary questions about the church.*

Our faith in the Church is not faith in the perfectness of the
human institution of which we are a part. Rather, it is faith in
the Holy Spirit, who bears witness to the things of God in and
through the Church, who continues to guide and correct God's

---

* *Crisis in Unity and Witness* (Philadelphia: Geneva Press, 1968),
Copyright © 1968 by the publisher, pp. 21 f. Used by permission.

rebellious and foolish people, so that we can assert with confidence that in spite of all its failings the Church is indeed the holy Church of the living God.

In preceding chapters, we have touched on some of the basic elements of the life of the fellowship of the Holy Spirit. These elements are much the same as in the description of the earliest Christian fellowship in the book of Acts: "They met constantly to hear the apostles teach, and to share the common life, to break bread, and to pray" (2:42, NEW ENGLISH BIBLE). The Church still hears the apostolic proclamation of Christ as it reads the Scriptures and listens to the preaching of its pastors; it still meets to share a common life, to receive the sacraments, and to offer its prayers.

These things are the work of the Holy Spirit, creating and renewing "The holy Catholic Church, The Communion of Saints," as the Apostles' Creed puts it; or the "one holy Catholic and Apostolic Church," as the Nicene Creed says.

In our day, the special gifts, or *charismata,* of the Holy Spirit to individual Christians are coming into prominence once again. As St. Paul says in I Corinthians 12: "To each is given the manifestation of the Spirit for the common good. To one is given through the Spirit the utterance of wisdom, and to another the utterance of knowledge according to the same Spirit, to another faith by the same Spirit, to another gifts of healing by the one Spirit, to another the working of miracles, to another prophecy, to another the ability to distinguish between spirits, to another various kinds of tongues, to another the interpretation of tongues. All these are inspired by the same Spirit, who apportions to each one individually as he wills" (Vss. 7-11).

The existence of such dramatic gifts is not confined to Pentecostalists. They are occasionally found among members of the churches in the Consultation and also among Roman

Catholics. But the real point of the Apostle was that every Christian has his own spiritual gifts, whether of a dramatic or an everyday character. He reminds the Corinthians that such gifts are for "the common good," and further that the gifts of leading and ordering the Church are also the work of God. "Now you are the body of Christ and individually members of it. And God has appointed in the church first apostles, second prophets, third teachers, then workers of miracles, then healers, helpers, administrators, speakers in various kinds of tongues" (Vss. 27, 28).

The whole life of the Church, and of each of its members, is energized and directed by the Holy Spirit. But just as the Holy Communion, the sacrament of unity, becomes the focal point of disunity, so the conviction that our Church life is the work of the Holy Spirit makes it difficult, if not impossible, for us to compromise our differences in doctrine, worship, sacraments, ministry, and church order. Each separate Christian communion believes that it has been brought by the Holy Spirit to the place where it is today. And who will say that the Spirit is an unreliable guide?

Yet, as an Orthodox archbishop once said, "The walls of separation do not reach up to heaven." These words of Metropolitan Platon of Kiev were taken up by Abbe Couturier, the saintly French Roman Catholic ecumenist of the difficult days before the Second Vatican Council, and became the theme of one of his annual tracts for the Church Unity Octave. In spite of its divisions, the Church remains the one Church of Christ, and, by the indwelling of the Spirit, continues to bring men into loving relationship with him.

Abbe Couturier, with the spiritual penetration which was characteristic of his work, wrote in a 1939 tract a paragraph which might provide the key to the problem of different understandings of truth attributed to the one Spirit:

It is no good dreaming that there will come *first* a realization of the unity of minds in Truth and *then* union of hearts in Charity. Truth is not to be apprehended save by a soul prepared to receive it, a soul already dedicated to it through a glimpse, however obscure, of desire and of love. Charity is the herald of Truth. The Word began by the charity and the humility of the Incarnation in order that in the form of the Servant he might win the hearts of men: the only means which he judged capable of obtaining the attention of their minds in freedom. Christians in their separation have no other model for their common work of mutual understanding, for all, Catholics included, are surrounded with darkness and ignorance of one another. . . .

It is clear enough that the unity desired by Christ is an organic unity such as will grasp and gather into his heart the soul of mankind in its entirety. The unity of Christians will then necessarily bring with it, athwart a great cultural diversity which it will harmonize, a unity of thought, of faith, of creed, since in all Christians it is the unique thought of their one Saviour which will develop itself. But that is the end and not the beginning.*

Charity, Christian love, is prior to doctrinal agreement. For as St. Paul says in I Corinthians 13, as the climax of his discourse on spiritual gifts it is the greatest gift of all. It is what makes the Christian fellowship a fellowship.

"Love never ends; as for prophecy, it will pass away; as for tongues, they will cease; as for knowledge, it will pass away. For our knowledge is imperfect and our prophecy is imperfect; but when the perfect comes, the imperfect will pass away." In these strikingly modern words, the Apostle underlines what is nowadays called the "historical conditioning" of our hearing of the word of God; all prophecies are partial, all knowledge is incomplete.

Accordingly, even our deepest Christian convictions must be held in the assurance that the Holy Spirit has yet more to

* Quoted in Geoffrey Curtis, *Paul Couturier and Unity in Christ* (London: SCM Press, 1964), pp. 98 f. Used by permission.

teach us of Christian truth; and it is quite possible that what he has said to other Christians from whom we have been separated is a part of what he intends us to learn.

The principal instrument of the Spirit for teaching Christian truth is, of course, the Holy Scriptures. As the United Presbyterian Confession of 1967 says, "The one sufficient revelation of God is Jesus Christ, the Word of God incarnate, to whom the Holy Spirit bears unique and authoritative witness through the Holy Scriptures, which are received and obeyed as the Word of God written. The Scriptures are not a witness among others but a witness without parallel."

Yet, one of the many ecumenical movements behind the ecumenical movement is the common discovery that, as this Confession goes on to state, the Scriptures "are nevertheless the words of men, conditioned by the language, thought forms, and literary fashion of the times and places at which they were written." And we who read them are also conditioned by our own historical situation, by the particular past through which we have gone and the setting in which we now live.

This does not mean that the Church wallows in a sea of universal doubt; on the contrary, its faith has remained fundamentally the same for nearly 2,000 years. But perhaps it does mean that particular systems of doctrine, conflicting with each other though fashioned from the same Scriptures by serious-minded and intelligent men, do not have the eternal and immutable validity which they were once thought by their partisans to have. As Pope John XXIII said, "The authentic teaching of the Church is to be studied and set forth according to the methods of research and the forms of expression which serve modern thinking. The substance of the old teaching comprehended in the deposit of faith is to be differentiated from the formulation in which it is clothed."

The contemporary guidance of the Holy Spirit is as necessary for understanding the Scriptures themselves as it was for the writing of the Scriptures; and one may assume that his guidance is directed to the chief purposes of his activity among men: the giving of life, of holiness, of wholeness, of unity in the faith and truth of Jesus Christ.

Even the word "truth" is a word of many meanings, meanings which spring from our own historical situation. For contemporary Americans it means an abstraction, a statement agreeing with the facts, but in earlier English use and in both the Old Testament and the New, it means trueness, faithfulness, constancy, fidelity. In the King James Version of John 3:21, the full force of Jesus' statement is conveyed better than in the modern versions: "But he that *doeth truth* cometh to the light, that his deeds may be made manifest, that they are wrought in God." This is the kind of truth into which the Holy Spirit leads us, that we may worship the Father "in spirit and in truth."

When a group of scientists gather to pool their knowledge of different disciplines toward the solution of a common problem, they are not compromising; they are learning from each other. Similarly, when scholars or ministers or lay people of different Christian traditions come together in the spirit of Christian love to share their experience of the things of God, they are not compromising but bearing witness to the work of the Holy Spirit as they have known it and learning new things about him from their fellow Christians.

Reaffirming an ancient, but neglected, principle, the Vatican Constitution on the Church declares: "The entire body of the Faithful, anointed as they are by the Holy One, cannot err in matters of belief. They manifest this special property by means of the whole people's supernatural discernment in matters of faith when 'from the Bishops down to the last of the lay faithful' they show universal agreement in matters of faith and morals. That discernment in matters of faith is aroused and sustained by the Spirit of truth."

While regarding nonpapal Christians as less than fully incorporated in the society of the Church, the Constitution notes many elements of common Christian life with them, adding: "Likewise we can say that in some real way they are joined with us in the Holy Spirit, for to them too he gives his gifts and graces, whereby he is operative among them with his sanctifying power." It appears that the darkness and ignorance of which Abbe Couturier spoke in 1939 are beginning to be dispelled.

If, with the Roman Catholics, we can recognize the sanctifying power of the Holy Spirit in the life of other Christian churches, there is really no insurmountable barrier remaining. "For all who are led by the Spirit of God are sons of God. For you did not receive the spirit of slavery to fall back into fear, but you have received the spirit of sonship. When we cry, 'Abba, Father!' it is the Spirit himself bearing witness with our spirit, that we are children of God" (Romans 8:14-16).

And the Apostle goes on with mounting enthusiasm: "What then shall we say to this? If God is for us, who is against us? . . . Who shall separate us from the love of Christ? Shall tribulation, or distress, or persecution, or famine, or nakedness, or peril, or sword? . . . No, in all these things we are more than conquerors through him who loved us. For I am sure that neither death, nor life, nor angels, nor principalities, nor things present, nor things to come, nor powers, nor height, nor depth, nor anything else in all creation, will be able to separate us from the love of God in Christ Jesus our Lord" (Vss. 31, 35, 37-39).

Differences in faith and order among the churches are, in considerable measure, the expression of differences in ways of thinking about the activity of the Holy Spirit in the Church.

Of the nine churches in the Consultation on Church Union, the one most fully representing the Catholic tradition is the Episcopal Church, and it shares what may be called the proprietary feeling about the Holy Spirit that is characteristic of that tradition. It is taken for granted that God will give the gift of the Spirit for confirmation, for the diaconate, for the priesthood, for the episcopate, in answer to the prayer of the Church with the laying on of the bishop's hands.

If it were assumed that God can be compelled to do such things against his will, this would of course be gross superstition. But the assumption is really just the opposite—that God wills these gifts for his people and is himself taking the initiative through those whom he has appointed and empowered to exercise the ministry of Christ. Strongly in this vein is the language of II Timothy 1:6: "Hence I remind you to rekindle the gift of God that is within you through the laying on of my hands" and with somewhat different emphasis, I Timothy 4:14: "Do not neglect the gift you have, which was given you by prophetic utterance when the elders laid their hands upon you."

It is generally agreed by scholars that these two epistles, with the Epistle to Titus, represent a relatively late strain of New Testament writing, after the death of the Apostle. (In those days an imaginary letter was not thought of as a forgery, but a respectable literary form.) But the earlier book of Acts gives ample attestation of the giving of gifts of the Spirit through the laying on of hands with prayer (8:14-17; 9:17-18; 13:1-3; 19:1-7). Though these occasions show a diversity of purpose and of detail, they all testify to the confidence of the early Christians that they were stewards of the mysteries of God, ministering the gift of the Spirit in his name.

In this rite, found in the Old Testament as well as the New, can be seen the beginnings of what evolved into the sacramental actions of confirmation and ordination which were thought of as peculiarly the responsibility of the bishops, the divinely appointed rulers and chief priests of the Church. Among Presbyterians, there are some who hold to the opinion that the presbytery is divinely established to rule the Church, others who consider it a human institution for the good ordering of the Church. Among Congregationalists, as the quotation from the Theological Commission of the United Church of Christ in Chapter VI suggests, the main locus of the authoritative action of the Holy Spirit lies in the local congregation.

In both traditions, ordination is thought of mainly as a public recognition and commissioning of those to whom God has given gifts suitable for ministry. The giving of these gifts is the direct act of God by the Holy Spirit, recognized by the Church rather than done through the Church.

Thus, the Book of Church Order of the Presbyterian Church in the U.S. says (Chapter 23-1): "Calling to office in the Church is the act of God by His Holy Spirit. This calling, ordinarily, is made manifest through the inward testimony of a good conscience on the part of the person, the approbation of God's people on the part of the Church, and the concurring judgment of a lawful court of the Church."

Then, in 23-4: "Ordination is the authoritative admission of one duly called to an office in the Church of God, accompanied with prayer and the laying on of hands, to which it is proper to add the giving of the right hand of Christian fellowship."

The solution of such differences as these rests in the mind of the Holy Spirit whom we all invoke as the lifegiver and renewer of the Church. It is easy to see why those who did not break with the church order of the Middle Ages continued to see in it a divinely chosen and empowered stewardship of the mysteries of God. It is also easy to see why those who felt that this ministry had been false to its stewardship rejected for both old bishop and new presbytery or congregation any attitude of proprietorship over the gifts of the Holy Spirit. In the Reformation period these issues were not merely the concern of learned theologians but of social groupings, political parties, and finally of armies drawn up in battle.

The subject of the ministry has already been discussed in Chapter VII. It is brought up again here as an example of the work of the Holy Spirit in the economy of salvation. Unquestionably the Catholic tradition needs correction when the stewardship of God's servants slides over into an attitude of proprietorship; it is strongly probable that contemporary styles in the relation of man to man require a new manner and spirit of exercising leadership in the Church as well as in other institutions of society. However, it may be equally important to recapture the faith that God does work in and through his Church and his ministers to bring his gifts to men. This is in line with the Pauline teaching that Christians should think of their pastors as ministers of Christ and stewards of the mysteries of God first and representatives of the congregation second.

Hans Küng, the brilliant Swiss Catholic theologian of renewal, puts the relationship between Spirit and Church in its true proportions:

Clearly one can understand the Church only if he understands the Spirit that moves the Church, moves it really and ultimately. Of course many spirits move the Church: good ones and bad ones —human spirits. Yet according to the belief of the Catholic Church and Christianity (in this Church but also in the other Christian churches), above all human spirits there is another whose power is altogether different, a mysterious, free Spirit: the Holy Spirit.

It would be dangerous to identify the Holy Spirit with the Church: the Holy Spirit is not the Church, but the Spirit of God. On that truth is based the fundamental *freedom* of the Holy Spirit.

Nowhere in the New Testament is the Holy Spirit called "Spirit of the Church," but always either "Spirit of God" or "Spirit of Jesus Christ." This Spirit emerges neither from the Church nor from the Christian, but only from God himself. He is not the bestowal and gift, the power and strength of the Church, but of God. He acts *on* the Church, manifests himself *to* the Church, comes *to* the Church, establishes and maintains the Church. But he does not become the Church's own spirit. He remains God's own Spirit. Therefore he is and remains the *free* Spirit.*

In any case it is plain that in disagreements among Christians, not all the health and truth are on one side and all the sin and heresy on the other. The answer must be found in a common search, in a spirit of love, for the leading of the Holy Spirit today. This approach, as has been pointed out in a variety of contexts, has worked wonders already in resolving many formerly hard-fought controversies; and if we do indeed believe that we all are led by the Spirit of God and are sons of God, who can stop us from arriving at a common mind in Christ?

> *Send your Holy Spirit into our hearts, Almighty God, heavenly Father, that he may direct and rule us according to your will, comfort us in all our afflictions, defend us from all falsehood and confusion, and lead us into all truth; through Jesus Christ our Lord, who lives and reigns with you and the same Spirit, one God, through endless ages. Amen.*

* *Freedom and Man*, ed. by John Courtney Murray, (New York: P. J. Kennedy, 1965); used by permission. Quoted in *Second Living Room Dialogues*, p. 238.

"All Places and All Ages"

What will the Church of tomorrow be like? Will the nine churches involved in the Consultation manage to solve all the problems of doctrine, worship, sacraments, and ministry that face them, agree on a structure for church government, and actually bring together their 25-million-member constituency in one religious body? And, if so, how long will it take?

Will the united Church so constituted fulfill its dream of being a uniting Church, eventually coming to agreement with Lutherans, Baptists, Eastern Orthodox, and Roman Catholics so that all in each place who are baptized into Jesus Christ and confess him as Lord and Saviour will actually be brought by the Holy Spirit into one full committed fellowship?

These are crystal-ball questions, of course, Nobody knows the answer, and it must be confessed that such a development seems almost impossible.

But the impossible has happened again and again in the relatively brief time that the ecumenical movement has been in existence. A generation ago, who could have forecast the amount of friendly intellectual interchange and common action that is taking place today among the Protestant, Anglican, and

Orthodox churches? Who would have dared to dream, even ten years ago, of the sweeping changes that have taken place within the Roman Catholic church and in its relationships with other forms of Christianity? There is no reason to expect the impossible to stop happening now.

One thing seems to be clear: everybody is a little bit more ecumenical this year than he was last year. There is something about the kind of world we live in that forces us to be open to our fellow men and to seek reconciliation and relationship with them. Whether it be the threat of nuclear war, the pains of the racial struggle, the impact of the technological explosion, or simply the inspiration of the Holy Spirit, we suddenly seem to be able to hear the call of the New Testament for a new world, a renewed humanity in Christ, as we have not heard it for the past several hundred years.

As to the speed with which union is likely to come, the representatives of the nine churches engaged in the Consultation clearly do not want any delay to be the result of their own failure to press forward on their part of the task—the development of a plan of union for study, consideration, and ultimate action by the several governing bodies. The 1968 meeting directed the executive committee to constitute a commission "to prepare the draft of a Plan of Union for submission to the Consultation not later than the 1969 meeting, if possible," but the reader is advised not to hold his breath until the draft is ready for submission to the churches.

There are great problems of church order still to be wrestled with: the Methodist system of clergy assignment by the bishop *vs.* the several varieties of call and acceptance used in other churches; the insistence of the United Church of Christ that no decision of the national governing body is binding on the local congregation (which can leave the union if it so decides); the necessary constitutional powers for the exercise of the office of bishop, together with the appropriate checks and balances upon those powers. These are just a few of the many unresolved issues.

Another point must be kept in mind: and that is that throughout Christian history there have been Christian sectarians alienated from the general body of the Church, who have preached the gospel to people alienated from the society. Even in the Gospel itself we are told of the man who cast out demons in Jesus' name but didn't consort with the disciples. Jesus told them, "Do not forbid him; for he that is not against you is for you" (Luke 9:50). Such Christians are, so to speak, the Lord's irregular troops, and they will always have a part to play in the proclamation of the gospel.

But the "regular" Christians—those who work together in all ways except religious ways, eat together in all places except where they feed upon the bread of life, talk and sing together on all themes except the praise of God—these are the ones who must face seriously the implications of Christ's prayer for unity among his followers.

And, indeed, this is already going on. Christians are starting to work together on projects designed to show forth Christ's concern for his people; they are meeting together occasionally to praise God; they are beginning to come together in Holy Communion even where to do so is a violation of church rules. The Christian community is discovering itself to be in existence, quite independently of anything that is being said or done in the Consultation on Church Union or in church administrative and legislative bodies.

It may truthfully be said that those working at the official level are struggling to provide a theological and canonical rationale for something that is already happening among church people rather than dreaming up a great project for an unprepared and uninterested constituency. That constituency, of course, includes all kinds of people, living in a variety of situations. There are some, particularly in stable communities in America's heartland, who simply have not been exposed to the winds of change and see no particular reason for a new religious alignment; but others, in communities of rapid change or in places where the impact of great world movements is felt, are readier to make bold experiments than the church leadership.

In spite of the intensity of human conflict in our time—perhaps because of it—the call to human unity is loud and insistent. Church unity may seem to some to be too small an objective to meet this tremendous need; indeed, it may seem to be at cross-purposes with the wider goal of peace and fellowship with all men—Jews, Muslims, Buddhists, Hindus, agnostics, atheists.

Christians do have to consider very seriously their role in ministering to this desperate need of mankind; they need to have a more profound appreciation of other faiths by which men live and of the men who live by these faiths. But if the Christian assessment of the nature of man is sound, if the Christian testimony to the saving mission of Christ is well founded, the gospel must go on being proclaimed with Christ at its center, for the sake of the world itself. Men can't undiscover atomic energy, even though it has been and may again be used very badly. And we can't undiscover Jesus, even though people have done, and may do again, terrible things in his name.

Dialogue with people of other faiths is certainly to be sought. In the U.S.A. this is particularly important with the Jewish community, which is closely related to Christianity, has suffered grievously in the recent past, and has a significant place on the American scene. But the purpose of such dialogue should never be to arrive at theological agreement. While many individual Jews have become Christians—several bishops of the Episcopal Church were of Jewish parentage—the Jewish community as a whole is another matter, and the dream of converting it can easily turn into a nightmare.

As Paul says in the eleventh chapter of Romans, "a hardening has come upon part of Israel, until the full number of the Gentiles come in, and so all Israel will be saved. . . . As regards the Gospel they are enemies of God, for your sake; but as regards election they are beloved for the sake of their forefathers. For the gifts and the call of God are irrevocable." So he takes "the conversion of the Jews" (union with the whole faith community) off the Christian agenda until the end of the world.

Religious dialogue with the Jews can be meaningful in many ways: to deepen our knowledge of the Old Testament; to enhance our understanding of the man Jesus, a faithful son of Israel; to discover common concerns and resources for meeting human need.

Christian evangelism, as D. T. Niles, the great Ceylonese Christian, has said, is "one beggar telling another beggar where to find bread." It is telling good news to those who are hungry for it. The hungry man may be a Jew, a Muslim, a Buddhist, or (quite often) a certified member of some Christian church. But he is not likely to be a committee or a dialogue group.

There may be a highly significant role for tomorrow's Church in dialogue with the great religions of the East—Islam, Buddhism, Hinduism. Christianity and Judaism are religions with a strong secular cast. They believe that God cares about what happens to people in this world, and find that his covenant with men is full of demands for the right ordering of personal and social relationships. The need for world peace and prosperity, of conditions providing a decent life for common people, and how our several religions interpret and minister to this need, would seem to be an urgent subject for inter-religious conversation.

That remarkably comprehensive document, the Second Vatican Council's Constitution on the Church, includes this paragraph (no. 16) on non-Christian religions:

Finally, those who have not yet received the Gospel are related in various ways to the people of God. In the first place, we must recall the people to whom the testament and the promises were given and from whom Christ was born according to the flesh. On account of their fathers this people remains most dear to God, for God does not repent of the gift he makes or the calls he issues. But the plan of salvation also includes those who acknowledge the Creator. In the first place, among these are the Mohammedans, who, professing to hold the faith of Abraham, along with us adore the one and merciful God, who on the last day will judge mankind. Nor is God far distant from those who in shadows and images seek the unknown God, for it is he who gives to all men life and breath and all things, and as Saviour wills that all men be saved. Those also can attain to salvation who through no fault of their own do not know the Gospel of Christ or His Church, yet sincerely seek God and moved by grace strive by their deeds to do his will as it is known to them through the dictates of conscience. Nor does divine providence deny the helps necessary to salvation to those who, without blame on their part, have not yet arrived at an explicit knowledge of God and with his grace strive to live a good life. Whatever good or truth is found amongst them is looked upon by the Church as a preparation for the Gospel. She knows that it is given by him who enlightens all men so that they may finally have life. But often men, deceived by the Evil One, have become vain in their reasonings and have exchanged the truth of God for a lie, serving the creature rather than the Creator. Or some there are who, living and dying in this world without God, are exposed to final despair. Wherefore, to promote the glory of

God and procure the salvation of all of these and mindful of the command of the Lord, "Preach the Gospel to every creature," the Church fosters the missions with care and attention.

Accordingly, in addition to appointing a postconciliar Secretariat for Christian Unity, the Vatican has appointed a Secretariat for Non-Christian Religions, and another for nonbelievers.

One real problem facing tomorrow's Church is its relationship with other churches around the world. Each of the nine bodies in the Consultation on Church Union is part of a worldwide fellowship of churches with similar traditions. Although these fellowships come together in consultative bodies rather than international organs of church government, they are real and meaningful nonetheless. It is universally agreed that it would be disastrous to arrive at a national unity within one country at the cost of losing the international unity of the several traditions—Anglican, Methodist, Reformed, Disciples of Christ.

Principles of Church Union, in its Preamble, emphasizes the importance of keeping up these international relationships to the fullest possible extent.

The unity of Christ's body is indivisible; to establish it locally at the expense of wider expressions of unity would defeat our purpose as certainly as would merely denominational or confessional unity, however widely spread across the world, defeat us in meeting our need of unity at home. We agree that our relationships to other bodies cannot remain separate and private matters, and that the united church itself, locally or in other appropriate units, must be the determining body. For example, relationships with existing world confessional bodies would be those of the united church, not of some continuing group within it. Again, membership in councils of churches—local, national, world-wide—would be in the name of the new body. In this our goal would be to add, to associations which formerly existed, a new fabric of associations which have hitherto been inaccessible to the separate churches and thus to extend through visible forms and vital experiences our solidarity with the people of God in all places and ages.

Even more to the point, perhaps, is the fact that the various churches in other countries with which American churches wish to maintain close relationships are almost all engaged in serious discussions looking toward unity with other churches—usually representatives of the same traditions that are found within the Consultation on Church Union. Some combination of Anglicans, Congregationalists, Methodists, and Presbyterians are engaged in unity discussions in England, Scotland, Wales, Ireland, Canada, Australia, New Zealand, India, Pakistan, Ceylon, the Arab countries, South Africa, Central Africa, East Africa, and West Africa.

As a practical matter, it would appear that the best way to stay in full communion with our fellow Christians in other parts of the world is to keep abreast of them as they develop their plans for union and put them into effect. Coordination to this end is being effected by the use of observers, the exchange of documents and papers, and most helpfully by the Consultation on Church Unity Negotiations held at Bossey in 1967. Even at international meetings of confessional bodies, reports and discussions of union plans are an important item on the agenda.

Since the real objective is the unity of the whole Christian fellowship (except for those vitally necessary "irregular Christians" previously mentioned), the union of a smaller grouping must be evaluated by its contribution to the greater goal. If we are to take the New Testament teaching on unity seriously, we should be in full Christian relationship with any other Christian group with which it is possible to be in such relationship. The burden of proof is always on those who wish to remain separate, because disunity is a denial of the nature of the one Church and a failure of Christian love. Nevertheless, it will be necessary for the Consultation to labor long and earnestly to make sure that tomorrow's Church is so Catholic that the Roman Catholics and Eastern Orthodox understand it to be so; so Evangelical that Baptists and Lutherans see and appreciate it as such, and so Reformed and reforming that it measures up to God's call for renewal in faithful service to him and his world.

But above all, tomorrow's Church must continue to be the Church of all places and all ages, like the scribe instructed in the kingdom of God, of whom Jesus spoke, who can bring out of his treasure things new and old. Our times are impatient of old things and old ways, and perhaps this is part of the sickness of our civilization, with its symptoms in moral decline, alienation of man from man, of generation from generation, and the aimless groping of men and groups for a sense of identity.

In a united Church it would seem important to remember and cherish the several pasts from which its members have come. Our true religious identity in each of these churches has not been in the brand name of the Church but in our being baptized communicant Christians, people in whom Christ dwells and who dwell in him. Nevertheless, we have all had particular ways of being Christian which God has blessed with his grace and power and presence.

Just as the American usually remembers with pride and affection the land from which his ancestors came, in a united Church we should be proud to be Episcopo-Christians, Methodo-Christians, and so on—Christians who have a past to remember thankfully and reverently as well as a present to embrace with joy. Everything vital to true obedience to Christ must be preserved in the united Church (if not, there will not be a united Church!), and within it there will be ample room for particular traditions that have meaning for particular groups. But what we shall have in common in tomorrow's Church will be far, far more than anything particular and individual.

Unless the Church can manifest its oneness in tomorrow's world it will condemn itself to futility and irrelevance to God and man. What a strange thought it is that our worship of the Lord of life, the Creator of all things, should turn us into people who rejoice in their differences from other worshipers of the same Lord! At one point in the development of Western civilization, perhaps this delight in our peculiarities made spiritual sense. As the common man emerged into full person-hood and discovered himself to be an individual, there was gospel in the fact that his individuality was uniquely expressed in his worship of God. But in a world that must choose between human brotherhood and total destruction, the good news of redemption must be expressed once more in the New Testament concept of organic unity of mankind in Christ.

"There is one body and one Spirit, just as you were called to the one hope that belongs to your call, one Lord, one faith, one baptism, one God and Father of all, who is above all and through all and in all" (Ephesians 4:4-7).

This one body consists of many members. Tomorrow's Church will be more varied in every way than the relatively homogeneous denominations that have gone into it. We shall need to understand the differing perspectives from which different people see life—the local congregation, the diocese or state, the general Church; the small town and the big city; varying economic levels. Rather than dismiss the relevance of one perspective to another, we should realize that we are all blind men trying to describe the elephant that one of us has by the tail, another by the trunk, another by the leg, while another touches its side.

Union of the nine churches in the Consultation on Church Union will bring about a racially integrated Church containing a larger proportion of Negroes than the general population. The participation of the black churches in this movement is not without cost, as the Episcopal Address of the African Methodist Episcopal Church indicates: "To the enraged militant, the role of mediator will often seem that of the traitor and the church—our church as well as all of the churches— must be prepared, for the crucifixion its faith teaches is at the heart of atonement" (see Appendix, p. 125).

And above all, the task of the Christian in tomorrow's world will be as it is today, to testify to his own faith, joyfully and without rancor. I believe in a heavenly Father who acts in this world, and who pleases to do so in response to prayer. I believe in his divine Son who came down to be one of us for our salvation. I believe that the fulfillment of his purpose lies not within the mundane existence of this planet or galaxy, but beyond it in a heavenly consummation. I believe in the Spirit who dwells in God's people in this world and seals us for the heavenly kingdom. I believe it is the will of the triune God that Christians should manifest his kingdom in this world by deeds of love, mercy, and justice to all men, individually and through the structures of society, so that men may know something of his nature and purpose. I believe that the only door into this kingdom is one that you must stoop to enter: knowing yourself to be a sinner, knowing your dependence on him, and receiving in the sacraments that which only he can give.

Having all these things, as his gift through his Church, why should we be angry at anybody? Why should we be worried about anything?

> *Gracious Father, we pray for your holy Catholic Church, that you will be pleased to fill it with all truth, in all peace. Where it is corrupt, purify it; where it is in error, direct it; where in anything it is amiss, reform it. Where it is right, establish it; where it is in need, provide for it; where it is divided, reunite it; for the sake of him who died and rose again, and always lives to make intercession for us, Jesus Christ, your Son, our Lord. Amen.*

APPENDIX:

Some Recent Statements on
Faith, Order, and Unity

This appendix consists mostly of a selection of statements from churches participating in the Consultation on Church Union on the subject of Christian faith and order and on their ecumenical commitment. The statements are reproduced here to give the reader an opportunity to sense the variety and vitality of the different traditions working together in the Consultation to shape a united Church that will be truly Catholic, truly Evangelical, and truly Reformed.

Also included are two significant statements embodying the results of dialogue between representatives of these traditions and Roman Catholics.

Together, these documents testify not only to variety but to a converging movement to recapture the central Christian Tradition, which is the heritage of all Christians, and ultimately of all mankind.

Our Mission–Today and Tomorrow

An excerpt from the Episcopal Address to the Quadrennial General Conference, 1968.

The African Methodist Episcopal Church is not the construct of human ambition. Its founders, prophets of the Most High God, saw clearly the apostasy of racism threatening American Christianity. Primitive Methodism, with its deep concern for the disinherited and oppressed, was a welcome haven for the African, both the free and the enslaved. But as it grew in numbers and in importance, its African membership became an embarrassment to its efforts to achieve status for itself in the Colonies. Moreover the widely held doctrine of the verbal inspiration of the Bible led the theologians of the period to seek accommodation with the Old Testament concept of a "chosen people." When the ambitions of this relatively unimportant tribe of Semites developed, so did the pretensions of their tribal god. Yahweh became the God of all the earth, but they were His "special" concern. The Gentile Christians of the early church dealt with this problem by substituting a culture for ethnology. The "chosen people" now were the followers of Jesus, not the descendants of Abraham, as the labored arguments of Romans and Hebrews reveal. But through the centuries, as Europe came to dominance in Christianity, the "chosen people" tended to recover its primitive ethnological connotation. When in North America, Christianity confronted the Indian and the African, it faltered. The true witness of the Gospel found expression in many individual Christians, but the institution —the church—failed the test. When Richard Allen and his followers left the service at St. George, that fateful Sunday in 1787, they did not separate themselves from Methodism or from St. George Church. It was as a member of St. George's Quarterly Conference, two years later, that Allen was ordained by Bishop Asbury a local deacon. It was, as a point on the circuit of which St. George was the head, that in 1784 Allen opened Bethel African Methodist Episcopal Church. Why did Allen wait 29 years—from 1787 to 1816, to create an independent church? A close study of the events shows clearly, I believe, that Allen was laboring to bring Methodism to re-assert its "Wesleyan inclusiveness," to save it from the trauma which overtook it, and from which it has not yet fully recovered.

It was the suit brought against him, in the courts of Pennsylvania that convinced Allen and his followers of the need for the separate organization of the African Methodist Episcopal Church. Thus it became the original "Black Power" movement in the country. The use of the word "African" in the name of the church was most meaningful. It served notice that Africans, without denying their identity, would claim for themselves every prerogative of humanity. It meant that they were convinced that the instrumentalities of their salvation must be forged by their own hands. We furnished the "shock troops" of the Abolition and the architects of the Reconstruction. We lifted the banner of Education and pointed a people, whom society had made it a crime to teach, to the open door of the class room.

But "Black Power" with the African Methodist Episcopal Church has always been a strategy and not an end. We do not seek any separate state or nation any more than we do a separate neighborhood. Our leaders did not support the "Back to Africa" movement of the American Colonization Society a century ago. America's problem is not Black Power, but White Power. It is "White Power" which, as Eli Ginzburg and Alfred S. Eichner point out in their recent book, "The Troublesome Presence," caused American presidents, from George Washington to William Howard Taft, to believe that the Negro had no future in America and ought to go back to Africa. Since the fateful day when a man, in that pitiful little band of courageous followers of James Meredith on his march through Mississippi, raised a clenched fist and shouted "Black Power," the guilty conscience of white America has reacted violently. For although she has rejected the descendants of the Africans in every area of her society, she is deeply disturbed at any prospect that they might look to any other people or country for deliverance or identity. Like any slogan, "Black Power," means many different things depending upon the person and the occasion of its use. Essentially, however, it is a cry of defiance to what President Johnson's Committee on the '67 riots calls "white racism." It symbolizes a drawing together in mutual recognition for self-defense and self-expression.

There have been instances where its response to a specific situation has been excessive; but every impartial government study in this field, from that of President Roosevelt's first Civil Rights Committee to President Johnson's Committee, has documented the fact that for over a hundred years the provocation has been grievous. In this situation the role of the African Methodist Episcopal Church is that of the Bridge. But a bridge must have strong moorings on each side of the chasm. Our identity with the oppressed and disinherited must be complete and unequivocal. Neither as individuals nor as an institution must the African Methodist Episcopal Church ever become an apologist for the injustices of the status quo, or urge the grateful acceptance of a grudging tokenism as a substitute for long overdue justice. A new sense of our poverty as a people must lead us to abandon wasteful displays of false affluence in favor of more self-sustaining economic policies. Many of our meetings could go back to our neighborhoods and our homes and facilities. Our congregations must be guided away from ill-considered building programs and equipment purchases which render the church impotent when the economic mobilization of the community is required. We ought to go on at once from talking to acting in the long sought merger of our three Methodist churches. This General Conference should declare its intention to this end and give its Commission power to begin during the ensuing Quadrennium by merging the membership and ministry of these three churches.

But to be a bridge, we must build equally strong moorings on the other side of the chasm. We must point out the false antithesis in the language of racism. In the program of God, there is no more basis for antagonism between black and white than between large people and small people, or tall people and short people. Man's true goal must not be the growth of "Black Power" or the destruction of "White Power." Our task is the increase of man, the growth of "Human Power," the perfection of humanity. This is the way Phillips brings out the impact of Paul's letter to Colossae, ". . . the full wonder and the splendor of (God's) secret plan for the nation. And the secret is simply this: Christ *in you!* Yes, Christ *in you* bringing with him the hope of all the glorious things to come." Thus our task is "to bring every man up to his full maturity." How those words to the Church at Ephesus illumine our situation and take on surprising relevancy. To the enraged militant, the role of the mediator will often seem that of the traitor and the church—our church as well as all of the churches—must be prepared, for the crucifixion its faith teaches is at the heart of atonement. God's gifts to us were made that Christians might be properly equipped for their service, that the whole body might be built up until the time comes, when in the unity of common faith and common knowledge of the Son of God, we arrive at real maturity—that measure of development which is meant by "the fullness of Christ." We are meant to hold firmly to "the truth in love," and to grow up every way into Christ, the Head. We are to work in the Local, State and National Councils of Churches. We are to be a functioning part of the ecumenical movement. Our membership in the Consultation on Church Union should be affirmed. The outstretched hand, not the closed fist or the raised palm should be our symbol. Like Edwin Markham, though another draws a circle to shut us out, we must have the wit to win, and draw a circle that takes him in. Our motto, which expresses the faith of our Church and the spirit of its founders, even if it was not formulated until years later, gives us the framework of our "bridge" even as it expresses the goal of our striving—"God, our Father; Christ, our Redeemer; Man, our Brother."

2. The Disciples of Christ

Faith and Polity

The general principles of faith and polity of the International Convention of Christian Churches (Disciples of Christ) are set forth in the following preamble to a Provisional Design for the Church, adopted by the Commission on Brotherhood Restructure for study, revision, and ultimate presentation to the General Assembly.

1. As members of the Christian Church, we confess that Jesus is the Christ, the Son of the living God, and proclaim him Lord and savior of the world. In his name and by his grace we accept our mission of witness and service to mankind. We rejoice in God our Father, maker of heaven and earth, and in the covenant of love by which he has bound us to himself. Through baptism into Christ we enter into newness of life and are made one with the whole people of God. In the fellowship and communion of the Holy Spirit we are joined to one another in brotherhood and in obedience to Christ. At the table of the Lord we celebrate with thanksgiving his saving acts and his presence. Within the universal church we receive the gift of ministry and the light of scripture. In the bonds of Christian faith we yield ourselves to God, that we may serve him whose kingdom has no end. Blessing, glory and honor be to him forever. Amen.

2. With the whole family of God on earth, the church appears wherever believers in Jesus Christ are gathered in his name. Transcending all barriers of race and culture, the church manifests itself in ordered communities of disciples bound together for worship, for fellowship and for service, and in varied structures for mission, witness and mutual discipline, and for the nurture and renewal of its members. The nature of the church, given by Christ, remains constant through the generations; yet in faithfulness to its mission it continues to adapt its structures to the needs and patterns of a changing world. All dominion in the church belongs to Jesus Christ, its Lord and head, and any exercise of authority in the church on earth stands under his judgment.

3. Within the universal body of Christ, the Christian Church (Disciples of Christ), manifests itself organizationally in free and voluntary relationships at congregational, regional and general levels. Each manifestation with reference to the function for which it is uniquely responsible, is characterized by its integrity, self-government, authority, rights and responsibilities. In the United States of America and in Canada, the Christian Church (Disciples of Christ), hereinafter generally referred to as the "Christian Church," is identifiable by its tradition, name, institutions and relationships. The Christian Church confesses Jesus Christ as Lord and constantly seeks in all its actions to be obedient to his authority.

4. In order that the Christian Church through free and voluntary relationships may faithfully express the ministry of Christ made known through scripture, may provide comprehensiveness in witness, mission and service, may furnish means by which congregations may fulfill their ministries with faithfulness in Christian stewardship, may assure both unity and diversity, and may advance responsible ecumenical relationships, as a response to God's covenant, we commit ourselves to one another in adopting this provisional design for the Christian Church (hereinafter referred to as "this design").

5. In keeping with this design the Christian Church shall: establish a General Assembly, a General Board and an Administrative Committee of the General Board; provide for such administrative units as may be required; provide for and act in and through related regional manifestations (hereinafter referred to as "regions"); establish, receive and nurture congregations; define procedures for the ordering of its ministry; develop or recognize new forms of ministries for mission, education and service; provide for appropriate consultation and interim procedures whereby existing organizations may make any necessary transition within the provisions of this design; and seek to provide for continuing renewal and reformation.

Documents on Church Unity

In voting to participate in the Consultation on Church Union, the 1964 General Convention of the Protestant Episcopal Church in the U.S.A. reaffirmed three earlier statements on church unity: The Chicago Quadrilateral, adopted by the House of Bishops in 1886; the Lambeth Quadrilateral of 1888, derived from the 1886 statement and given additional weight as a statement of a conference of bishops of the whole Anglican Communion around the world; and a Statement of Faith and Order approved by the General Convention of 1949 for use in discussions on church unity. The texts follow:

THE CHICAGO QUADRILATERAL

WHEREAS, Many of the faithful in Christ Jesus among us are praying with renewed and increasing earnestness that some measures may be adopted at this time for the re-union of the sundered parts of Christendom:

NOW, THEREFORE, in pursuance of the action taken in 1853 for the healing of the divisions among Christians in our land, and in 1880 for the protection and encouragement of those who had withdrawn from the Roman Obedience, we, Bishops of the Protestant-Episcopal Church in the United States of America, in Council assembled as Bishops in the Church of God, do hereby solemnly declare to all whom it may concern, and especially to our fellow-Christians of the different Communions in this land, who, in their several spheres, have contended for the religion of Christ:

1. Our earnest desire that the Saviour's prayer, "That we all may be one," may, in its deepest and truest sense, be speedily fulfilled;

2. That we believe that all who have been duly baptized with water, in the name of the Father, and of the Son, and of the Holy Ghost, are members of the Holy Catholic Church;

3. That in all things of human ordering or human choice, relating to modes of worship and discipline, or to traditional customs, this Church is ready in the spirit of love and humility to forego all preferences of her own;

4. That this Church does not seek to absorb other Communions, but rather, co-operating with them on the basis of a common Faith and Order, to discountenance schism, to heal the wounds of the Body of Christ, and to promote the charity which is the chief of Christian graces and the visible manifestation of Christ to the world;

But furthermore, we do hereby affirm that the Christian unity now so earnestly desired by the memorialists can be restored only by the return of all Christian communions to the principles of unity exemplified by the undivided Catholic Church during the first ages of its existence; which principles we believe to be the substantial deposit of Christian Faith and Order committed by Christ and his Apostles to the Church unto the end of the world, and therefore incapable of compromise or surrender by those who have been ordained to be its stewards and trustees for the common and equal benefit of all men.

As inherent parts of this sacred deposit, and therefore as essential to the restoration of unity among the divided branches of Christendom, we account the following, to wit:

1. The Holy Scriptures of the Old and New Testament as the revealed Word of God.

2. The Nicene Creed as the sufficient statement of the Christian Faith.

3. The two Sacraments,—Baptism and the Supper of the Lord,—ministered with unfailing use of Christ's words of institution and of the elements ordained by Him.

4. The Historic Episcopate, locally adapted in the methods of its administration to the varying needs of the nations and peoples called of God into the unity of His Church.

FURTHERMORE, Deeply grieved by the sad divisions which affect the Christian Church in our own land, we hereby declare our desire and readiness, so soon as there shall be any authorized response to the Declaration, to enter into brotherly conference with all or any Christian Bodies seeking the restoration of the organic unity of the Church, with a view to the earnest study of the conditions under which so priceless a blessing might happily be brought to pass.

(Note: While the above form of the Quadrilateral was adopted by the House of Bishops, it was not enacted by the House of Deputies, but rather incorporated in a general plan referred for study and action to a newly created joint Commission on Christian Reunion.)

LAMBETH CONFERENCE OF 1888

RESOLUTION II

That, in the opinion of this Conference, the following Articles supply a basis on which approach may be by God's blessing made towards Home Reunion:—

(a) The Holy Scriptures of the Old and New Testaments, as "containing all things necessary to salvation," and as being the rule and ultimate standard of faith.

(b) The Apostles' Creed, as the Baptismal Symbol; and

the Nicene Creed, as the sufficient statement of the Christian faith.

(c) The two Sacraments ordained by Christ Himself—Baptism and the Supper of the Lord—ministered with unfailing use of Christ's words of Institution, and of the elements ordained by Him.

(d) The Historic Episcopate, locally adapted in the methods of its administration to thë varying needs of the nations and peoples called of God into the Unity of His Church.

STATEMENT OF FAITH AND ORDER

THE QUADRILATERAL

A. The Holy Scriptures

The Holy Scriptures are the inspired record of God's self-revelation to man and of man's response to that revelation. This is the primary ground of the authority of the Scriptures.

The fact that the Church under the guidance of the Holy Spirit has accepted the Bible as canonical invests it as a whole with an authoritative character for all Christians. Its authority is further validated by the continuing experience of Christian people.

The Bible has an inner unity as the record of the special preparation for Christ, and of His redemption of man through His Life, Death, Resurrection, and Ascension, and through the gift of the Holy Ghost. Both in the Old and in the New Testaments the Kingdom of God is proclaimed and everlasting life is offered to mankind in Christ, the only Mediator between God and Man.

The Bible has been and is for the Christian Church the ultimate criterion of its teaching and the chief source of guidance for its life. It contains all doctrine required for salvation through faith in Jesus Christ.

The reading and preaching of the Word of God are indispensable for the life and worship of the Church.

B. The Creeds

The Apostles' Creed rehearses the mighty acts of God in creation, redemption, and sanctification as recorded in the Holy Scriptures. Upon these, the life of the Church is based. As a declaration of allegiance to the Triune God the Apostles' Creed is a profession of Faith appropriate to Holy Baptism.

The Nicene Creed likewise witnesses to the faith of the historic Church in its assertion of fundamental Christian truths and its denial of fundamental errors and is appropriate to Holy Communion.

While liberty of interpretation may be allowed, the Christian faith as set forth in these two creeds ought to be received and believed by all Christian people.

The recitation of the Creeds in public worship is to be commended, though their invariable use in such fashion is not essential to the unity or the life of the Church.

C. The Sacraments

Baptism with water and with the Spirit, in the Name of the Father and of the Son and of the Holy Ghost, is a divinely instituted sacrament whereby we are made children of grace and incorporated into the Church, and receive forgiveness of sin and a new birth unto righteousness. The requirements for baptism are repentance and faith, declared by the recipient or on his behalf by his sponsors.

The Supper of the Lord, ministered with unfailing use of Christ's words of institution and the elements ordained by Him, is the supreme act of sacramental worship in the Christian

Church. This Sacrament is a corporate act of the Church towards God, wherein it is united with its Lord, victorious and triumphant, Himself both Priest and Victim in the sacrifice of the Cross. In it the faithful continue a perpetual memory of the precious death of Christ who is their Advocate with the Father and the propitiation for their sins, according to His precept, until His coming again. For the first they offer the sacrifice of praise and thanksgiving; then next they plead and represent before the Father the sacrifice of the Cross, and by it they confidently entreat remission of sins and all other benefits of the Lord's passion for all the whole Church; and lastly they offer the sacrifice of themselves to the Creator of all things which they have already signified by the oblations of the bread and wine which are His creatures. In the Supper of the Lord the faithful receive and partake, spiritually, of the Body and Blood of Christ; and thus enter into communion with Christ Himself and with one another in His Life.

In addition to the sacraments of Baptism and the Supper of the Lord, the Church recognizes sacramental rites or mysteries, namely, Confirmation, Absolution, the Marriage Blessing, Holy Orders and the Unction of the Sick.

D. The Historic Episcopate

1. THE MINISTRY. The fundamental Christian ministry is the ministry of Christ. There is no Christian priesthood or ministry apart from His. His priestly and ministerial function is to reconcile the world to God in and through Himself, by His Incarnation and by His "one sacrifice once offered" and by the gift of the Holy Spirit, delivering men from the power of sin and death.

The Church as the Body of Christ, sharing His life, has a ministerial function derived from that of Christ. In this function every member has his place and share according to his different capabilities and calling. The Church is set before us in the New Testament as a body of believers having within it, as its recognized focus of unity, of teaching and of authority, the Apostolate, which owed its origin to the action of the Lord Himself. There was not first an Apostolate which gathered a body of believers about itself; nor was there a completely structureless collection of believers which gave authority to the Apostles to speak and act on its behalf. From the first there was the fellowship of believers finding its unity in the Twelve. Thus the New Testament bears witness to the principle of a distinctive ministry, as an original element, but not the sole constitutive element, in the life of the Church.

2. THE EPISCOPATE. Anglican formularies deal with the episcopate as a fact rather than a doctrine. It is, however, a fact deeply rooted in history. The Lambeth Quadrilateral is, accordingly, employing a defining phrase when it speaks of the "historic episcopate." Acceptance of episcopacy as a basis of reunion necessarily means acceptance of it not as a bare fact, but a fact accompanied by its historical meaning.

The maintenance of a ministerial succession, by way of ordination with the laying on of hands, is a familiar fact in the life of most Christian communions. All such ministerial successions are in some sense historic, differing from one another, however, in form and in the degree to which succession is continuous in history. Anglican formularies pronounce no judgments on other ministerial successions. They do claim, however, for the churches of the Anglican Communion for which they speak, that these churches have preserved both the form and the succession which traces back to the "Apostles' time," and they make the preservation of this succession a matter of scrupulous discipline. They define ministers within this historic stream as "Ministers of Apostolic Succession."

It should be clear, therefore, that while acceptance of the "historic episcopate" may not involve acceptance of any one formulation of the doctrine of the ministry, it does involve acceptance, in the form of a fact, of the three-fold ministry of bishops, priests, and deacons, and the acceptance of it also as accompanied by the claim that it is a ministerial succession tracing back to the "Apostles' time."

The Lambeth Conference Report of 1930 enlarges upon this claim as follows:

When we speak of the Historic Episcopate, we mean the Episcopate as it emerged in the clear light of history from the time when definite evidence begins to be available. . . . Without entering into the discussion of theories which divide scholars, we may affirm shortly that we see no reason to doubt the statement made in the Preface to our Ordinal that 'from the Apostles' time there have been these Orders of Ministers in Christ's Church: Bishops, Priests and Deacons.' Whatever variety of system may have existed in addition in the earlier age, it is universally agreed that by the end of the second century episcopacy had no effective rival. Among all the controversies of the fourth and fifth centuries the episcopal ministry was never a subject of dispute. . . . If the Episcopate, as we find it established universally by the end of the second century, was the result of a process of adaptation and growth in the organism of the Church, that would be no evidence that it lacked divine authority, but rather that the life of the Spirit within the Church had found it to be the most appropriate organ for the functions which it discharged. In the course of time the Episcopate was greatly affected by secular forces, which bent it to many purposes alien to its true character and went far to obscure its spiritual purpose. . . . The Historic Episcopate as we understand it goes behind the perversions of history to the original conception of the Apostolic Ministry.

The concept of the episcopate can, accordingly, receive definition as an historical fact. It can also receive clarification from a description of its functions.

To quote from the Lambeth Report of 1930:

When we say that we must insist on the Historic Episcopate but not upon any theory or interpretation of it, we are not to be understood as insisting on the office apart from the functions. What we uphold is the Episcopate, maintained in successive generations by continuity of succession and consecration, as it has been throughout the history of the Church from the earliest times, and discharging those functions which from the earliest times it has discharged.

When we refer to the historic episcopate we are concerned with the essentials and purposes of the office of bishop and not with the incidental attributes of the office or the details of the administration of the Church, which have changed from time to time and may continue to change.

The most obvious function of the "historic episcopate"—the one which in the course of its varied history, has been most scrupulously guarded—is its vocation of transmitting the ministerial succession. The bishop is thus the organ of ministerial continuity. He is also the personal organ of the Church's unity. The very name bishop (episcopos) implies the function of pastoral care, of oversight. He is addressed in the Church's traditional liturgies as Father-in-God. He is also addressed as the Church's Shepherd. He represents the Church catholic to his flock, as the localized minister cannot do. Expressive of the Bishop's function of ministering the Word and of pastoral oversight is the opening prayer of the Anglican *Form of Ordaining or Consecrating a Bishop.*

Almighty God, who by thy Son Jesus Christ didst give to thy holy Apostles many excellent gifts, and didst charge them to feed thy flock; Give grace, we beseech thee, to all Bishops, the Pastors of thy Church, that they may diligently preach thy Word, and duly administer the godly Discipline thereof.

The fourth point of the Lambeth Quadrilateral was rephrased by the Lambeth Conference of 1920, in its *Appeal to All Christian People,* as follows:

A ministry acknowledged by every part of the Church as possessing not only the inward call of the Spirit, but also the commission of Christ and the authority of the whole Body.

We close this section by further quoting from this *Appeal*:

May we not reasonably claim that the Episcopate is the one means of providing such a ministry? It is not that we call in question for a moment the spiritual reality of the ministries of those Communions which do not possess the Episcopate. On the contrary, we thankfully acknowledge that these ministries have been manifestly blessed and owned by the Holy Spirit as effective means of grace. But we submit that considerations alike of history and of present experience justify the claim which we make on behalf of the Episcopate. Moreover, we would urge that it is now and will prove to be in the future the best instrument for maintaining the unity and continuity of the Church. But we greatly desire that the office of a Bishop should be everywhere exercised in a representative and constitutional manner, and more truly express all that ought to be involved for the life of the Christian Family in the title of Father-in-God. Nay more, we eagerly look forward to the day when through its acceptance in a united Church we may all share in that grace which is pledged to the members of the whole body in the apostolic rite of the laying-on-of-hands, and in the joy and fellowship of a Eucharist in which as one Family we may together, without any doubtfulness of mind, offer to the one Lord our worship and service.

3. THE PRIESTHOOD AND THE DIACONATE. The office of a priest (presbyter) is to minister to the people committed to his care; to preach the Word of God; to baptize; to celebrate the Holy Communion; to pronounce absolution, or remission of sins, and blessing in God's name. Thus he exercises part of the Apostolic office, and it is significant that in the Anglican Ordinals, as in the general practice of the Western Church, which is itself based on very early usage, priests are associated with the Bishop in laying on of hands at the ordination of priests.

The office of a deacon is to assist the priest in divine service, and in his other ministrations, under the direction of the bishop. In the early Church the diaconate represented the ministry of the Church to men's bodily needs, but not as though these were separable from their spiritual states. Though this function is still emphasized in Anglican Ordinals, the deacon today exercises his office almost entirely in spiritual activities.

4. LAITY. To the whole Church of God and to every member of it belongs the duty and privilege of spreading the good news of the Kingdom of God and the message of salvation through Jesus Christ and of interceding for the brethren. All, according to their measure, share in the priesthood which the Church derives from Him. This is the meaning of the doctrine of the priesthood of all believers.

THE QUADRILATERAL AND THE CHURCH

We have confined our exposition to the Quadrilateral; its interpretation must be seen in the context of the scriptural doctrine of the Church. This involves more extended consideration than can be given in this statement. We can, however, join with other Christian bodies in the affirmation in the Edinburgh report on *Faith and Order:*

We are at one in confessing belief in the Holy Catholic Church. We acknowledge that through Jesus Christ, particularly through the fact of His resurrection, of the gathering of His disciples round their crucified, risen, and victorious Lord, and of the coming of the Holy Spirit, God's Almighty will constituted the Church on earth.

The Church is the people of the new covenant, fulfilling and transcending all that Israel under the old covenant foreshadowed. It is the household of God, the family in which the fatherhood of God and the brotherhood of man is to be realized in the children of His adoption. It is the body of Christ, whose members derive their life and oneness from their one living Head; and thus it is nothing apart from Him, but is in all things dependent upon the power of salvation which God has committed to His Son.

The presence of the ascended Lord in the Church, His Body, is effected by the power of the one Spirit, who conveys to the whole fellowship the gifts of the ascended Lord, dividing to every man severally as He will, guides it into all the truth and fills it unto all the fulness of God.

We all agree that Christ is present in His Church through the Holy Spirit as Prophet, Priest, and King. As Prophet He reveals the divine will and purpose to the Church; as Priest He ever liveth to make intercession for us, and through the eternal sacrifice once offered for us on Calvary He continually draws His people to the Most High; and as King He rules His Church and is ever establishing and extending His Kingdom.

Christ's presence in the Church has been perpetual from its foundation, and this presence He makes effective and evident in the preaching of the Word, in the faithful administration of the Sacraments, in prayer offered in His name, and through the newness of life whereby

He enables the faithful to bear witness to Himself. Even though men often prove faithless, Christ will remain faithful to the promise of His presence, and will so continue till the consummation of all things.

CONCLUSION

The foregoing statement is not a complete formulation of the faith and order of the Church. It is an exposition of the background and chief implications of the Chicago-Lambeth Quadrilateral. It has been formulated, not as a final pronouncement to which literal subscription should be asked, but as a means of assuring a substantial agreement upon the basis of which formal schemes for Church Union with any other Church may later be drawn up. We hope that the document will form a useful instrument of further negotiation with those Christian bodies which may be willing to join with us in seeking a way into that unity to which our Lord is calling all Christian people.

4. *The Presbyterian Church in the United States*

A Brief Statement of Belief

This contemporary statement of belief was adopted by the Southern Presbyterian Church in 1962, not as amending older formularies but "to present in the language of our time the historic Christian doctrine set forth in Scripture and affirmed by the Presbyterian Church," with the recognition that "no statement of Christian doctrine can ever be final or complete."

GOD AND REVELATION

The living and only true God has made himself known to all mankind through nature, mind, conscience, and history. He has especially revealed himself and his purpose for man in the variety of ways recorded in the Old and New Testaments. The Bible, as the written Word of God, sets forth what God has done and said in revealing his righteous judgment and love, culminating in Christ. The Spirit of God who inspired the writers of Scripture also illumines readers of Scripture as they seek his saving truth. The Bible calls men to an obedient response to the Gospel and is the supreme authority and indispensable guide for Christian faith and life.

God has revealed himself as the Creator, Sustainer, and Ruler of all that exists. In the exercise of his sovereign power in creation, history, and redemption, God is holy and perfect, abundant in goodness, and the source of all truth and freedom. He is just in his dealings with all the world; he requires that men live and act in justice; and he visits his wrath on all sin. He is gracious and merciful and does not desire that any should perish. Both his judgments and his mercies are expressions of his character as he pursues his redemptive purposes for man.

God is personal and he reveals himself as the Trinity of Father, Son, and Holy Spirit. It is the witness of the Scriptures, confirmed in Christian experience, that the God who creates and sustains us is the God who redeems us in Christ, and the God who works in our hearts as the Holy Spirit; and we believe that this threefold revelation manifests the true nature of God.

MAN AND SIN

God created man in his own image. As a created being, man is finite and dependent upon his Creator. Man can distinguish between right and wrong, and is morally responsible for his own actions. He reflects the image of God insofar as he lives in obedience to the will of God. A unique creature standing both within nature and above it, he is placed by God in authority over the world. It is, therefore, his responsibility to use all things for the glory of God. Although made in the image of God, man has fallen; and we, like all mankind before us, sin in our refusal to accept God as sovereign. We rebel against the will of God by arrogance and by despair. We thrust God from the center of life, rejecting divine control both of human life and the universe. From this perversity arises every specific sin, whether of negligence, perfunctory performance, or outright violation of the will of God.

Sin permeates and corrupts our entire being and burdens us more and more with fear, hostility, guilt and misery. Sin operates not only within individuals but also within society as a deceptive and oppressive power, so that even men of good will are unconsciously and unwillingly involved in the sins of society. Man cannot destroy the tyranny of sin in himself or in his world; his only hope is to be delivered from it by God.

CHRIST AND SALVATION

God, loving men and hating the sin which enslaves them, has acted for their salvation in history and especially through his covenant people. In the fullness of time, he sent his only, eternally begotten Son, born of the Virgin Mary. As truly God and truly man, Jesus Christ enables us to see God as he is and man as he ought to be. Through Christ's life, death, resurrection, and ascension, God won for man the decisive victory over sin and death and established his Kingdom among men. Through Christ, bearing on the cross the consequences of our sin, God exposed the true nature of sin as our repudiation of God. Through Christ, bearing on the cross the guilt of our sin, God forgives us and reconciles us to himself. By raising his Son from the dead, God conquers sin and death for us.

God has an eternal, inclusive purpose for his world, which embraces the free and responsible choices of man and everything which occurs in all creation. This purpose of God will surely be accomplished. In executing his purpose, God chooses men in Christ and calls forth the faith which unites them with Christ, releasing them from bondage to sin and death into freedom, obedience, and life. Likewise God in his sovereign purpose executes judgment upon sinful man.

Man cannot earn or deserve God's salvation but receives it through faith by the enabling power of the Holy Spirit. In faith, man believes and receives God's promise of grace and mercy in Christ, is assured of his acceptance for Christ's sake in spite of his sinfulness, and responds to God in grateful love and loyalty.

In repentance, man, through the work of the Holy Spirit, recognizes himself as he is, turns from his sin, and redirects his life increasingly in accordance with God's will. The Christian life is a continuing process of growth which reaches its final fulfillment only in the life to come.

THE CHURCH AND THE MEANS OF GRACE

The true Church is the whole community, on earth and in heaven, of those called by God into fellowship with him and with one another to know and do his will. As the body of Christ, the Church on earth is the instrument through which God continues to proclaim and apply the benefits of his redemptive work and to establish his Kingdom.

The Church in the world has many branches, all of which are subject to sin and to error. Depending on how closely they conform to the will of Christ as head of the Church, denominations and congregations are more or less pure in worship, doctrine, and practice. The Presbyterian Church follows scriptural precedent in its representative government by elders (presbyters). These elders govern only in courts of regular gradation. The form of government of a church, however, is not essential to its validity. The visible church is composed of those who profess their faith in Jesus Christ, together with their children.

Through the Church, God provides certain means for developing the Christian mind and conscience and for maturing faith, hope, and love. Primary among these means are the preaching, teaching, and study of the Word; public and private prayer; and the sacraments.

The Bible becomes a means of grace through preaching, teaching, and private study, as the Holy Spirit speaks to human needs and reveals the living Word of God who is Jesus Christ. It illuminates man's thought and experience as it provides an occasion for the Holy Spirit's work of redemption and as it testifies to the working of God, but it is not intended to be a substitute for science and inquiry. In preaching and teaching, the Church proclaims and interprets the mighty acts of God in history and seeks to relate them to every phase of human life. The prayerful and diligent study of the Scripture guides the Christian in his relationships with God and his fellow man, and in his personal life.

Christian prayer is communion with God in the name of Jesus Christ through the inspiration and guidance of the Holy Spirit. In prayers, alone or with others, we acknowledge God's greatness and goodness, confess our sins, express our love to him, rejoice in his blessings, present our needs and those of others, receive from him guidance and strength, and joyfully dedicate ourselves to his will. To pray in the name of Christ, our Mediator, is not to repeat a formula, but to trust his redemptive work, to ask for his intercession, to depend upon his presence with us and to desire what he has taught us to value and believe.

Christ gave to the Church through his apostles the sacraments of Baptism and the Lord's Supper as visible signs and assurances of the Gospel. Baptism sets forth, by the symbolic use of water, the cleansing and regenerating love of God through the work of the Holy Spirit; in this sacrament we and our children are assured that we are members of the covenant family of God, and are publicly accepted into fellowship with Christ and his Church. The Lord's Supper sets forth, by the symbolic use of bread and wine, the death of Christ for our salvation; in this sacrament we have communion with the risen Christ, who gives himself to us as we receive in faith the bread and wine for the nourishment of our Christian life. Being assured of his forgiving and sustaining love, we renew our dedication and enjoy fellowship with the whole people of God. The Lord's table is open to members of all churches who have publicly professed Jesus Christ as Saviour and Lord and who come in penitence and faith.

CHRISTIAN LIFE AND WORK

Each Christian is called to be a servant of God in all of life, so that we must seek God's will for the work we do and for the manner in which we do it. Christian vocation may be found in any work where our own abilities and interests best meet the legitimate needs of God's world. The Church is charged under God with the obligation to seek out the most responsible and effective Christian leadership. It is the special role of the ordained ministry, including elders and deacons, to perform particular services in the life of the Church and to strength every Christian in the discharge of the responsibilities of the priesthood of all believers in the Church and the world. For the Christian, all life becomes significant as he does his daily work with dedication and diligence out of love for God and for his neighbor.

The range of Christian responsibility is as wide as human life. The Christian must recognize, but not accept as inevitable, the world as it is, distorted and torn by sin. Christians as individuals and as groups have the right and the duty to examine in the light of the Word of God the effects on human personality of social institutions and practices. As servants of the sovereign will of God, Christians are under obligation to their fellow men and to unborn generations to shape and influence these institutions and practices so that the world may be brought more nearly into conformity with the purpose of God for his creation. The Church's concern for the reign of God in the world is essential to its basic responsibility both for evangelism and for Christian nurture.

We believe that our destiny and that of the world are not subject to chance or fate, but to the just and loving sovereignty of God. In this assurance we face the problems of suffering and evil. Faith in the purpose and providence of God assures us of his presence in suffering and of his power to give it meaning. We are confident that no form of evil can separate us from the love of

God, that God works in all things for good, and that evil will ultimately be overcome. Therefore, while we cannot fully understand the pain and evil of the present world, we can offer ourselves as active instruments of God's will in their conquest.

JUDGMENT AND THE LIFE TO COME

Eternal life is the gift of God. We are assured by the promises of the Gospel, by our relation to Christ, and by his resurrection that death does not put an end to personal existence, but that we too shall be raised from the dead. Those who have accepted the forgiving love of God in Christ enter into eternal life in fellowship with God and his people. This new life begins in the present world and is fulfilled in the resurrection of the body and the world to come. Those who have rejected the love of God bring upon themselves his judgment and shut themselves outside the fellowship of God and his people.

As Christ came once in humility, he will return in glory for the final judgment and for the consummation of his universal Kingdom. The work and promises of Jesus Christ give assurance that the age-long struggle between sin and grace will in God's good time have an end; all the power of evil will be destroyed, and God's holy, wise, and loving purposes will be accomplished.

5. The United Church of Christ

Faith, Purpose, and Mission

The Statement of Faith of the United Church of Christ was adopted by the 1959 General Synod of this church, a union of the Congregational-Christian and Evangelical and Reformed Churches. The commentary, by Dr. Roger Hazleton, is taken from a pamphlet, "The United Church of Christ: History and Program," produced by the United Church Board for Homeland Ministries. Of more limited sponsorship than the Statement of Faith, but trustworthy in its description of the church's life, is the Statement of Purpose and Mission adopted by its committee on structure in 1967.

THE STATEMENT OF FAITH

We believe in God, the Eternal Spirit, Father of our Lord Jesus Christ and our Father, and to his deeds we testify:

*He calls the worlds into being,
    creates man in his own image,
    and sets before him the ways of life and death.*

*He seeks in holy love to save all people from aimlessness
    and sin.*

*He judges men and nations by his righteous will
    declared through prophets and apostles.*

In Jesus Christ, the man of Nazareth, our crucified and
   risen Lord, he has come to us
   and shared our common lot,
   conquering sin and death
   and reconciling the world to himself.

He bestows upon us his Holy Spirit,
   creating and renewing the Church of Jesus Christ,
   binding in covenant faithful people of all ages,
      tongues, and races.

He calls us into his Church
   to accept the cost and joy of discipleship,
   to be his servants in the service of men,
   to proclaim the gospel to all the world
   and resist the powers of evil,
   to share in Christ's baptism and eat at his table,
   to join him in his passion and victory.

He promises to all who trust him
   forgiveness of sins and fullness of grace,
   courage in the struggle for justice and peace,
   his presence in trial and rejoicing,
   and eternal life in his kingdom which has no end.

Blessing and honor, glory and power be unto him. Amen.

COMMENTARY ON THE STATEMENT

Several years before the United Church of Christ was formed, the commission to prepare a statement of faith for the new church began its work. We had many meetings, a lot of discussion, made several attempts, and finally presented the Statement which is now in use to the Synod meeting at Oberlin in 1959. For some of us, it is not too much to say, the United Church of Christ really began that day as we confessed our faith together and spontaneously sang the Doxology. While we had to wait until the new constitution was adopted for the new church to become a legal, official fact, it was the Statement of Faith that gave life to the church in our thoughts and hearts. From then on we knew we belonged together and would stay together.

There have been some problems since that time, problems of getting better acquainted, of working out detailed arrangements, or of interpreting necessary changes. But the Statement of Faith has helped to make these problems easier to solve, because it brings the right perspective, that of Christian faith itself, into our wrestling with them. We are becoming more and more familiar with the Statement in church services, in conferences of laymen or ministers, and in study groups. It has already made a sure place for itself in our common work and life.

However, a brief introduction, or re-introduction, may be in order. First, *why* do we have this Statement of Faith? Are there not enough creeds, confessions, covenants as it is? Perhaps; but most of these speak the language of yesterday, not today. Although we may honor them as part of our Christian heritage, they do not necessarily speak *for* us as much as they speak *to* us. To some of us, at least, it seems important that each generation in the churches should re-think and then re-phrase its faith. It will certainly do us no good to go on parroting the past, as if the present did not exist and the future did not matter. Not that we should suppose it either possible or desirable to improve upon the Apostles' Creed, for example; but alongside it we need to place an affirmation of our own which sets forth what being Christian means to us and not to some long-past time. If we are able to make *the* faith in some degree *our* faith, then ought we not to find words to say what indeed has happened?

The Statement of Faith is our church's way of answering this question. Some day it too will be out of date, but right now it is the latest, freshest affirmation of our common belief. If a few of the words in it seem to have a rather musty odor, that is because Christianity was not born yesterday or the day before; Christians have been living with words like "judgment," "reconciliation," "eternal life," and "kingdom" for a very long time. Yet the accent is new even if all the words are not or cannot be, as you will discover when reading over the Statement thoughtfully.

What is this accent? In other words—and this is our second question—where does the Statement of Faith put its weight? Two things stand out, I think, with special clearness. One is that where the historic creeds say "I believe" this Statement says "We believe" instead. Here Christian faith is not a private matter, but a shared experience nurtured within the church. This is no loyalty oath or trap set to catch a heretic, but believing is seen in the perspective of belonging—to one another in the church because of what God does for us in Christ. The Statement of Faith, as we often say, is "a testimony, not a test" of faith.

Another striking feature of this new accent is that we are not talking about ourselves or even about the quality of our belief, but rather about God who inspires our belief. "To his deeds we testify"—that is, we are not propagandists or salesmen but only witnesses. And the God to whom we are witnessing is above all else a Doer, active and outgoing, who calls the worlds into being and ourselves into his kingdom. What is more, God's deeds are those of love itself, as Jesus taught and showed us, seeking us out, sharing with us, promising us forgiveness, courage, and companionship. Certainly this is putting the Christian accent in the right place.

And now, a third question: What use shall we make of the Statement of Faith? Doubtless it will continue to be said aloud by congregations, whether frequently or seldom, as an act of worship. Indeed its structure and phrasing were chosen with just this use in mind; notice how the sentences are broken up into short, concise segments, always with God as the subject, and the whole goes not meandering but marching on, like the Bible from Genesis to Revelation.

But this public use will be more meaningful, of course, if the Statement of Faith has been read and studied beforehand. You are invited to make use of it in this way. Think of it, as you read, as a banner of thoughtful allegiance carried at the head of the church's procession through time and space, blazoning forth our deepest needs and highest hopes as members of the Christian community. Do not ask, at first, whether you agree with all of it or not; but let it simply stir your interest and kindle your imagination. Then, when you are next invited to join in saying it in public worship, the Statement of Faith will come to have for you the worth and meaning that it was designed to provide.

ROGER HAZLETON, *Dean*
The Oberlin Graduate School of Theology

STATEMENT OF PURPOSE AND MISSION OF THE UNITED CHURCH OF CHRIST

FINAL REVISION—JANUARY 20, 1967

This Statement was prepared for the use and guidance of the Committee on Structure. It does not purport to express the views of the United Church of Christ or any part thereof other than the Committee on Structure.

The United Church of Christ was formed, according to the preamble to its Constitution, "in order to express more fully the oneness in Christ of the churches composing it, to make more effective their common witness in Him, and to serve His kingdom in the world." Although that is true, it is so inclusive that it fails to suggest the shape and style of the church to which it refers. As the Committee on Structure pursues its assignment to study services and interrelationships in the United Church in order to make its structure more effective, we must be clear about its character and its mission. It is a church of pioneering spirit which seeks to serve God in terms which are relevant to the changing times. Form and structure are essential, but from time to time they will change and may even die. They must always be subservient to mission.

United by our allegiance to Jesus Christ, we take for ourselves the purpose to be his witnesses, to proclaim the gospel, to make disciples of all nations, and to work for peace in the world, for justice among men, and for the acknowledgment of God's sovereignty over all. The commission is from God; the field of action is the world and all its people. The tasks to be undertaken and the methods to be employed take shape both in loyalty to Christ and in response to the changing world. It is the inevitable and indispensable tension between that loyalty and that response which makes it both difficult and imperative to define the purpose and program of the United Church.

It is our purpose through worship, stewardship, education, and evangelism to celebrate the presence of God in life, to sustain and strengthen a community of faith, and to equip its members for mission.

It is our purpose through witness, service, influence, and action to declare that God is at work in the world and to be his servants in the service of men, to meet human need, to undergird institutions of freedom, to preserve human values, and to effect the social change required to secure justice and freedom for all men.

It is our purpose through reflection, research, experimentation, and review to discover the needs of a changing world and to develop ministries to meet them, not in disregard of the past or in affection for novelty itself, but to serve God's purpose in the present and to break new trails of obedience into the future.

It is our purpose through ecumenical councils, consultations on union, and partnership in action to work for unity wherever possible and to continue to be a uniting as well as a united church, not because we trust in strength of numbers, but because we disavow sectarianism and seek the most effective way to do God's will in the world.

Since both our knowledge of God's will and our understanding of men's needs are imperfect, there are natural differences in judgment and in expression among those who share a common Christian loyalty. Therefore, the United Church of Christ means to provide room for the sincere witness of Christian believers who may differ widely in their understanding of God's will in specific situations. The Church must provide for corporate actions which its responsible bodies may take but must respect the integrity of those who dissent and the right of individuals to dissociate themselves from such actions.

The United Church consists of local churches, Associations, Conferences, General Synod, and the various Instrumentalities. Neither the national bodies, the Conferences, nor the Associations exercise authority over a local church. The local church is the basic unit of the United Church. The Associations, Conferences, and national bodies are created or recognized as instruments of mission. The United Church includes them all in a fellowship of freedom and responsibility, and all of them together bear mutual responsibility for the whole mission.

For its structure and program the United Church relies, not on hierarchal authority, but on full and effective. communication between the several parts so that each one can make its decisions in the light of its responsibility to and for the whole. The achievement of its purposes requires a structure of interrelationships which provides freedom through order, flexible enough to accommodate differences of understanding in a democratic process of decision-making yet strong enough to assure mutual support and faithfulness. The authority of the whole is the self-imposed willingness of each part to co-operate with the rest and to undergird and support the responsible leadership of those who represent the larger fellowship. The structure of the United Church needs to be more clearly defined in order to deepen the sense of loyalty and to strength the financial support of and by the several parts. Associations, Conferences, national bodies, and the specialized ministries which are provided should be seen as the outreach of local churches, and each local church and specialized ministry should be understood as the expression of the whole Church in its particular community.

The Cause of Christian Unity

This bench-mark of ecumenical commitment by the United Methodist Church was adopted by the Uniting Conference in Dallas, April 29, 1968; brought together were the Methodist Church and the Evangelical United Brethren. Correspondence is welcomed by the Commission on Ecumenical Affairs, 1200 Davis Street, Evanston, Illinois 60201.

Because "there is but one body and one Spirit, only one hope of God's calling, one Lord, one faith, one baptism, one God and Father of us all, who is above all and through all and in all" (Ephesians 4:4-6), it follows that the profoundest imperative to Christian unity springs from God's own design and providence for his covenant people. Yet another imperative, equally urgent, springs from the demand of the honest and faithful acceptance of God's gift of unity: the discrepancy between the Gospel we proclaim and the divisions we exhibit. This amounts to a contradiction. Increasingly in our time, the call to unity is made more urgent by our awareness that a divided Christendom is a hindrance to the effective mission of the Christian Church in the modern world.

The United Methodist Church willingly acknowledges these imperatives and reaffirms its resolute commitment to all feasible and valid measures to give them practical force and effect [cf.

Constitution, Par. V]. To this end, we pledge our continued participation in the ecumenical movement at all levels and also our concurrent efforts toward reform and renewal within our own church life in anticipation of the hazards and hopes of our ecumenical future under God.

We realize that the first phase of fruitful ecumenism is the mutual acquaintance of Christians developed across denominational lines. We commend this venture to our Methodist people as their ecumenical opportunity and obligation. We should earnestly seek the acquaintance of other Christians, on their terms, open to and appreciative of the contributions which their beliefs and practices can make to us. By the same token, we should cordially invite other Christians to make their acquaintance with us and to come to understand our distinctive ways and emphases. And yet we must be prepared for the practical consequences that may flow from such experiences: new demands that arise from unhindered fellowship in love, from more effective cooperation in common service, more meaningful worship together. These all point beyond themselves to deeper and more complete unity "in sacred things."

"Unity in the Spirit" is, therefore, the first, crucial stage of ecumenical initiation, but it is only a threshold on the way to authentic community in Christ. The fuller reality of such community has been hopefully described by the Third Assembly of the World Council of Churches at New Delhi (1961) in an important statement which we affirm as consonant with our own convictions:

We believe that the unity which is both God's will and his gift to his Church is being made visible as all in each place who are baptized into Jesus Christ and confess him as Lord and Savior are brought by the Holy Spirit into one fully committed fellowship, holding the one apostolic faith, preaching the one Gospel, breaking the one bread, joining in common prayer, and having a corporate life reaching out in witness and service to all and who at the same time are united with the whole Christian fellowship in all places and all ages in such wise that ministry and members are accepted by all, and that all can act and speak together as occasion requires for the tasks to which God calls his people.[1]

We take this to mean that the decisive goal of ecumenism is the unification of membership and ministries, to the end that amidst the diversity and pluralism that belong to the true genius of Christian community, Christians can worship and witness in a truly inclusive fellowship, without the indignities of rebaptism, reconfirmation, and reordination. It would also mean that our memberships and ministries would be reconciled and that all who are one in Christ could share in the joys and graces of full communion, each with all the others.

It is our solemn resolve to continue in quest of such unity and to be guided in our efforts to this end by the spirit and intent of the following propositions:

1. All those who are baptized with water and in the Triune Name, who confess Jesus Christ as Lord and Savior, who congregate to hear God's Word rightly preached and to receive Christ's sacraments duly administered, who serve the Great Commission (Matthew 28:19-20) in word and deed, and whose lives manifest God's ministry of reconciliation in Christ (II Corinthians 5:18-20) are members of Christ's Body, the Church (I Corinthians 12:27), and truly "members one of another" (Ephesians 4:25).

2. The unity we seek is the communion of all Christians in each place in the undeniable essentials of Christian life and discipline, among which we would include the following: the authority of God's revealed Word in Holy Scripture, the governance of the Church by the Holy Spirit, the Gospel of faith preached and heard and lived, a universal membership nurtured toward Christian maturity by the sacraments of grace and the

[1] *The New Delhi Report, The Third Assembly of the World Council of Churches, 1961* (New York: Association Press, 1962), "Unity," Par. 2, p. 116.

fellowship of service, the nurture of Christians in each new generation by the Christian tradition, a representative ministry ordained for the sacramental and pastoral guidance of the pilgrim People of God, an ethic of disciplined love that bears witness to God's design for love and justice in and for the whole human family. Diversities in doctrines, cults, ritual and polity that do not corrupt or disintegrate this essential core of community are not only allowable but actually welcome.

3. The United Methodist Church seeks to become part of a united Christian church that is truly *catholic* (universal, inclusive, faithful to the Christian tradition), truly *evangelical* (emphatic about justification by faith and zealous in its proclamation) and truly *reformed* (submissive to God's judgments, open to renewal by the Holy Spirit). Such a church must have rejected all barriers of race, sex, class and culture; it must be intensely missionary; it must be open to needful change in polity, liturgy of doctrinal formulation; it must be in the world and for the world: the servant of all those for whom Christ died.

4. We see in none of the existing churches, as they now exist, the perfect exemplar of the fullness of the Christian community we seek. This means that the path of ecumenical progress is not by "return," or absorption and even less by simple merger. Rather, we seek genuine further development on the part of all the communions concerned, aimed at an eventual convergence at some point still hidden in God's providence, when the divided churches will be enabled to combine their offerings to the common treasury and humbly abandon their erstwhile claims to self-sufficiency. But it also means that, in the interim, each church will move as directly and as far as possible toward such a convergence, so as to hasten the day of recovered unity and to prepare for its coming.

5. The United Methodist Church recognizes in the ecumenical movement a providential agency in aid of unity and it welcomes its provisions for appropriate occasions and processes

whereby separated churches can emerge from their self-contain-
ment and confront each other in an atmosphere of mutual trust,
mutual repentance and reform. Our constant danger is to settle
for the first-fruits of dialogue—i.e., "unity in the Spirit" and
Christian cooperation—and therefore to relax the urgency of its
constant *prime* objective: the recomposition of the Christian
community by means of the reunification of membership and
ministries. Ecumenism is not an end in itself. Endless ecumenical
dialogue becomes self-deceiving and self-defeating: self-deceiving
because it masks the dangers of our persisting disunity, self-defeating because talk of union without negotiations to achieve it is
bound to reinforce the mood of cynicism already apparent in the
world and in the churches, as to our ecumenical good faith. We
are convinced that, just as we have moved from diatribe to dialogue, so now we must move from dialogue to decision—in the
interest of honesty and effective mission. This involves our dealings
with our separated Christian brethren: it also involves our relationships with our separated brethren of other faiths.

6. The United Methodist Church understands itself as included within the covenanted People of God and cherishes its
share of the rich and variegated heritage bequeathed it from the
Christian past. We seek to identify ourselves within the mainstream of historic Christianity, in both its catholic and evangelical
aspects; we seek to be reformed and reforming. But we are also
conscious of our own "distinctive witness" within the larger scope
of the Christian tradition: an especial stress on "holiness of heart
and life," on the witness of the Holy Spirit in the mystery of salvation, on grace as prevenient, justifying and sanctifying, on
"good works" as needful evidence of authentic faith, on a con-
nectional system and an appointive principle in settling ministers,
on the efforts to seek the transformation of society through the
powers of the Christian ethic of faith, freedom and love. We do not
expect these emphases to be ignored but, rather, to see their good
essence caught up and conserved in a fuller manifestation of the

Christian tradition. The acid test of all such "distinctive emphases" in an age such as ours is their practical usefulness in the tasks of Christian witness and services. The most obvious import of this principle is that it will encourage development and reform at all levels throughout the church.

7. The United Methodist Church has and cherishes long-standing ties with other churches in its "family tradition," in this country and in other countries around the world. We intend, therefore, to continue our participation in and support of the World Methodist Council in its efforts to strengthen the bonds of fellowship between Methodists everywhere—not in a clannish spirit but with an eye to the richer contributions such collaboration may offer to our eventual union with Christians of other family traditions. At the same time, we also have and treasure long-term commitments to united national churches in several countries and we are resolved to maintain these relationships, involving as they may multiple patterns of interconnection. We would regard as inadequate any ecumenical proposals that would repudiate these cherished ties and relations.

8. The churches that united to form the United Methodist Church had a long history of sustained and vigorous participation in the conciliar network of ecumenical cooperation: in the Federal Council of the Churches of Christ in the U.S.A. (since 1908), the World Council of Churches (since 1948), the National Council of the Churches of Christ in the U.S.A. (since 1950), and in various state and local councils and associations. At the world level, we have profited from our involvement in the work of the International Missionary Council and in the various programs of the World Council of Churches, both in "Life and Work" and in "Faith and Order." At the national level, we have learned much from our work in the National Council of Churches about the problems and possibilities of cooperative service in the current crises of our modern cities and the problems posed by the vast sociological and technological developments that are changing the

face, and mind, of rural America. At state and local levels, we have learned much of what we know now about the cooperative services of Christians "in each place" and of the difficulties and hopes of effecting a Christian presence in secular society. We therefore reaffirm our intention to continue and strengthen our participation in, and support for, the conciliar movement (local, state, national, regional, world). We are mindful, of course, that no council has any immediate jurisdiction in any of our own affairs and that the mandate to all such councils is that they may indeed speak *to* the churches and *with* the churches, but not *for* them. Even so, we are ready to do our part in framing and sustaining their programs and in attending to their "messages" in a spirit substantially supportive and yet responsibly critical.

9. The churches now united in the United Methodist Church were long-time partners in the Consultation on Church Union and, here again, we intend to continue and to intensify our efforts in this undertaking, moving from mere consultation concerning "principles" to active negotiation in the preparation of A Plan of Union. In such a process it is the responsibility of the Council of Bishops and the Commission on Ecumenical Affairs to insure our competent representation in all the discussions and the referral of all substantive proposals back to the church and its conferences for review and assessment. It is also their duty to promote the widest possible process of education in ecumenism throughout the church, so that broadly representative decisions can be arrived at without undue delay.

10. We realize that serious planning for any larger unity involves expectation of actual change in our own accustomed ways and habitual practices. This suggests the relevance and urgency of deliberate self-examination of these ways and practices in the light of Scripture, Tradition, and the needs of modern man. This will obviously disclose real needs for reformation and reformulation and for creative experiments in theology, liturgy, discipline and polity. In such a self-examination it is essential that all available

resources throughout the church be enlisted, deployed and utilized—including our own faculties of theology and the wider theological community to which they belong. In such an undertaking, the United Methodist Church affirms her loyalty to the ancient motto, *ecclesia semper reformanda* ("the church in perennial reformation"), and pledges her best efforts at all levels to bold ventures in this spirit.

In their Second Vatican Council and afterward, our Roman Catholic brethren have learned a lesson from which we, too, can greatly profit. "There can be no ecumenism worthy of the name without a change of heart. It is from new attitudes toward others, from self-denial and unstinted love, that yearnings for unity take their rise and grow toward maturity . . . This change of heart and holiness of life, along with public and private prayer for the unity of all Christians, should be regarded as the soul of the whole ecumenical movement . . ."(*On Ecumenism,* Par. 7-8).

The real danger in the vigorous tides of ecumenical thought and action today is not the risk of change but the equally unhelpful extremes of the passionate fear of change and the reckless desire for change at any price. All of us are justified in seeking to bring our gifts into the wider union but not in rejecting or minimizing the gifts which the others have to bring. We must, therefore, cultivate open and expectant attitudes toward the prospects of actual ecumenical progress, convinced that the unity which is God's gift and Christ's command will strengthen our witness to Christ's love for men and his lordship in the world—that the world may come to hear and heed the Gospel.

The Confession of 1967 *

*The Book of Confessions of 1967 of the United Presbyterian
Church in the U.S.A. begins with the Nicene Creed and the
Apostles' Creed and continues with a series of historic statements of faith up to the Theological Declaration of Barmen
adopted by German Protestants in 1934 in opposition to Hitler's
church policies. It concludes with the following contemporary
statement.*

PREFACE

The church confesses its faith when it bears a present witness to
God's grace in Jesus Christ.

In every age the church has expressed its witness in words and
deeds as the need of the time required. The earliest examples of
confession are found within the Scriptures. Confessional statements
have taken such varied forms as hymns, liturgical formulas, doctrinal definitions, catechisms, theological systems in summary, and
declarations of purpose against threatening evil.

Confessions and declarations are subordinate standards in the
church, subject to the authority of Jesus Christ, the Word of God,
as the Scriptures bear witness to him. No one type of confession

---

* This text was approved by the 178th General Assembly (1966) as a
part of the proposal to revise the confessional position of The United
Presbyterian Church in the United States of America.

is exclusively valid, no one statement is irreformable. Obedience to Jesus Christ alone identifies the one universal church and supplies the continuity of its tradition. This obedience is the ground of the church's duty and freedom to reform itself in life and doctrine as new occasions, in God's providence, may demand.

The United Presbyterian Church in the United States of America acknowledges itself aided in understanding the gospel by the testimony of the church from earlier ages and from many lands. More especially it is guided by the Nicene and Apostles' Creeds from the time of the early church; the Scots Confession, the Heidelberg Catechism, and the Second Helvetic Confession from the era of the Reformation; the Westminster Confession and Shorter Catechism from the seventeenth century; and the Theological Declaration of Barmen from the twentieth century.

The purpose of the Confession of 1967 is to call the church to that unity in confession and mission which is required of disciples today. This Confession is not a "system of doctrine," nor does it include all the traditional topics of theology. For example, the Trinity and the Person of Christ are not redefined but are recognized and reaffirmed as forming the basis and determining the structure of the Christian faith.

God's reconciling work in Jesus Christ and the mission of reconciliation to which he has called his church are the heart of the gospel in any age. Our generation stands in peculiar need of reconciliation in Christ. Accordingly this Confession of 1967 is built upon that theme.

THE CONFESSION

In Jesus Christ God was reconciling the world to himself. Jesus Christ is God with man. He is the eternal Son of the Father, who became man and lived among us to fulfill the work of reconciliation. He is present in the church by the power of the Holy Spirit to continue and complete his mission. This work of God, the Father, Son, and Holy Spirit, is the foundation of all confessional statements about God, man, and the world. Therefore the church calls men to be reconciled to God and to one another.

PART I: GOD'S WORK OF RECONCILIATION

SECTION A. THE GRACE OF OUR LORD JESUS CHRIST

1. Jesus Christ

In Jesus of Nazareth true humanity was realized once for all. Jesus, a Palestinian Jew, lived among his own people and shared their needs, temptations, joys, and sorrows. He expressed the love of God in word and deed and became a brother to all kinds of sinful men. But his complete obedience led him into conflict with his people. His life and teaching judged their goodness, religious aspirations, and national hopes. Many rejected him and demanded his death. In giving himself freely for them he took upon himself the judgment under which all men stand convicted. God raised him from the dead, vindicating him as Messiah and Lord. The victim of sin became victor, and won the victory over sin and death for all men.

God's reconciling act in Jesus Christ is a mystery which the Scriptures describe in various ways. It is called the sacrifice of a lamb, a shepherd's life given for his sheep, atonement by a priest; again it is ransom of a slave, payment of debt, vicarious satisfaction of a legal penalty, and victory over the powers of evil. These are expressions of a truth which remains beyond the reach of all theory in the depths of God's love for man. They reveal the gravity, cost, and sure achievement of God's reconciling work.

The risen Christ is the savior for all men. Those joined to him by faith are set right with God and commissioned to serve as his reconciling community. Christ is head of this community, the church, which began with the apostles and continues through all generations.

The same Jesus Christ is the judge of all men. His judgment

discloses the ultimate seriousness of life and gives promise of God's final victory over the power of sin and death. To receive life from the risen Lord is to have life eternal; to refuse life from him is to choose the death which is separation from God. All who put their trust in Christ face divine judgment without fear, for the judge is their redeemer.

2. The Son of Man

The reconciling act of God in Jesus Christ exposes the evil in men as sin in the sight of God. In sin men claim mastery of their own lives, turn against God and their fellow men, and become exploiters and despoilers of the world. They lose their humanity in futile striving and are left in rebellion, despair, and isolation.

Wise and virtuous men through the ages have sought the highest good in devotion to freedom, justice, peace, truth, and beauty. Yet all human virtue, when seen in the light of God's love in Jesus Christ, is found to be infected by self-interest and hostility. All men, good and bad alike, are in the wrong before God and helpless without his forgiveness. Thus all men fall under God's judgment. No one is more subject to that judgment than the man who assumes that he is guiltless before God or morally superior to others.

God's love never changes. Against all who oppose him, God expresses his love in wrath. In the same love God took on himself judgment and shameful death in Jesus Christ, to bring men to repentance and new life.

SECTION B. THE LOVE OF GOD

God's sovereign love is a mystery beyond the reach of man's mind. Human thought ascribes to God superlatives of power, wisdom, and goodness. But God reveals his love in Jesus Christ by showing power in the form of a servant, wisdom in the folly of the cross, and goodness in receiving sinful men. The power of God's love in Christ to transform the world discloses that the Redeemer is the Lord and Creator who made all things to serve the purpose of his love.

God has created the world of space and time to be the sphere of his dealings with men. In its beauty and vastness, sublimity and awfulness, order and disorder, the world reflects to the eye of faith the majesty and mystery of its Creator.

God has created man in a personal relation with himself that man may respond to the love of the Creator. He has created male and female and given them a life which proceeds from birth to death in a succession of generations and in a wide complex of social relations. He has endowed man with capacities to make the world serve his needs and to enjoy its good things. Life is a gift to be received with gratitude and a task to be pursued with courage. Man is free to seek his life within the purpose of God: to develop and protect the resources of nature for the common welfare, to work for justice and peace in society, and in other ways to use his creative powers for the fulfillment of human life.

God expressed his love for all mankind through Israel, whom he chose to be his covenant people to serve him in love and faithfulness. When Israel was unfaithful, he disciplined the nation with his judgments and maintained his cause through prophets, priests, teachers, and true believers. These witnesses called all Israelites to a destiny in which they would serve God faithfully and become a light to the nations. The same witnesses proclaimed the coming of a new age, and a true servant of God in whom God's purpose for Israel and for mankind would be realized.

Out of Israel God in due time raised up Jesus. His faith and obedience were the response of the perfect child of God. He was the fulfillment of God's promise to Israel, the beginning of the new creation, and the pioneer of the new humanity. He gave history its meaning and direction and called the church to be his servant for the reconciliation of the world.

SECTION C. THE COMMUNION OF THE HOLY SPIRIT

God the Holy Spirit fulfills the work of reconciliation in man. The Holy Spirit creates and renews the church as the community in which men are reconciled to God and to one another. He enables them to receive forgiveness as they forgive one another and to enjoy the peace of God as they make peace among themselves. In spite of their sin, he gives them power to become representatives of Jesus Christ and his gospel of reconciliation to all men.

1. The New Life

The reconciling work of Jesus was the supreme crisis in the life of mankind. His cross and resurrection become personal crisis and present hope for men when the gospel is proclaimed and believed. In this experience the Spirit brings God's forgiveness to men, moves them to respond in faith, repentance, and obedience, and initiates the new life in Christ.

The new life takes shape in a community in which men know that God loves and accepts them in spite of what they are. They therefore accept themselves and love others, knowing that no man has any ground on which to stand except God's grace.

The new life does not release a man from conflict with unbelief, pride, lust, fear. He still has to struggle with disheartening difficulties and problems. Nevertheless, as he matures in love and faithfulness in his life with Christ, he lives in freedom and good cheer, bearing witness on good days and evil days, confident that the new life is pleasing to God and helpful to others.

The new life finds its direction in the life of Jesus, his deeds and words, his struggles against temptation, his compassion, his anger, and his willingness to suffer death. The teaching of apostles and prophets guides men in living this life, and the Christian community nurtures and equips them for their ministries.

The members of the church are emissaries of peace and seek

the good of man in cooperation with powers and authorities in politics, culture, and economics. But they have to fight against pretensions and injustices when these same powers endanger human welfare. Their strength is in their confidence that God's purpose rather than man's schemes will finally prevail.

Life in Christ is life eternal. The resurrection of Jesus is God's sign that he will consummate his work of creation and reconciliation beyond death and bring to fulfillment the new life begun in Christ.

2. The Bible

The one sufficient revelation of God is Jesus Christ, the Word of God incarnate, to whom the Holy Spirit bears unique and authoritative witness through the Holy Scriptures, which are received and obeyed as the word of God written. The Scriptures are not a witness among others, but the witness without parallel. The church has received the books of the Old and New Testaments as prophetic and apostolic testimony in which it hears the word of God and by which its faith and obedience are nourished and regulated.

The New Testament is the recorded testimony of apostles to the coming of the Messiah, Jesus of Nazareth, and the sending of the Holy Spirit to the Church. The Old Testament bears witness to God's faithfulness in his covenant with Israel and points the way to the fulfillment of his purpose in Christ. The Old Testament is indispensable to understanding the New, and is not itself fully understood without the New.

The Bible is to be interpreted in the light of its witness to God's work of reconciliation in Christ. The Scriptures, given under the guidance of the Holy Spirit, are nevertheless the words of men, conditioned by the language, thought forms, and literary fashions of the places and times at which they were written. They reflect views of life, history, and the cosmos which were then current. The church, therefore, has an obligation to approach the Scriptures with literary and historical understanding. As God has spoken his word in diverse cultural situations, the church is confident that he will continue to speak through the Scriptures in a changing world and in every form of human culture.

God's word is spoken to his church today where the Scriptures are faithfully preached and attentively read in dependence on the illumination of the Holy Spirit and with readiness to receive their truth and direction.

PART II: THE MINISTRY OF RECONCILIATION

SECTION A. THE MISSION OF THE CHURCH

1. Direction

To be reconciled to God is to be sent into the world as his reconciling community. This community, the church universal, is entrusted with God's message of reconciliation and shares his labor of healing the enmities which separate men from God and from each other. Christ has called the church to this mission and given it the gift of the Holy Spirit. The church maintains continuity with the apostles and with Israel by faithful obedience to his call.

The life, death, resurrection, and promised coming of Jesus Christ has set the pattern for the church's mission. His life as man involves the church in the common life of men. His service to men commits the church to work for every form of human well-being. His suffering makes the church sensitive to all the sufferings of mankind so that it sees the face of Christ in the faces of men in every kind of need. His crucifixion discloses to the church God's judgment on man's inhumanity to man and the awful consequences of its own complicity in injustice. In the power of the risen Christ and the hope of his coming the church sees the promise of God's renewal of man's life in society and of God's victory over all wrong.

The church follows this pattern in the form of its life and in the method of its action. So to live and serve is to confess Christ as Lord.

2. Forms and Order

The institutions of the people of God change and vary as their mission requires in different times and places. The unity of the church is compatible with a wide variety of forms, but it is hidden and distorted when variant forms are allowed to harden into sectarian divisions, exclusive denominations, and rival factions.

Wherever the church exists, its members are both gathered in corporate life and dispersed in society for the sake of mission in the world.

The church gathers to praise God, to hear his word for mankind, to baptize and to join in the Lord's Supper, to pray for and present the world to him in worship, to enjoy fellowship, to receive instruction, strength, and comfort, to order and organize its own corporate life, to be tested, renewed, and reformed, and to speak and act in the world's affairs as may be appropriate to the needs of the time.

The church disperses to serve God wherever its members are, at work or play, in private or in the life of society. Their prayer and Bible study are part of the church's worship and theological reflection. Their witness is the church's evangelism. Their daily action in the world is the church in mission to the world. The quality of their relation with other persons is the measure of the church's fidelity.

Each member is the church in the world, endowed by the Spirit with some gift of ministry and is responsible for the integrity of his witness in his own particular situation. He is entitled to the guidance and support of the Christian community and is subject to its advice and correction. He in turn, in his own competence, helps to guide the church.

In recognition of special gifts of the Spirit and for the ordering of its life as a community, the church calls, trains, and authorizes

certain members for leadership and oversight. The persons quali-
fied for these duties in accordance with the polity of the church
are set apart by ordination or other appropriate act and thus made
responsible for their special ministries.

The church thus orders its life as an institution with a constitution, government, officers, finances, and administrative rules.
These are instruments of mission, not ends in themselves. Different
orders have served the gospel, and none can claim exclusive
validity. A presbyterian polity recognizes the responsibility of all
members for ministry and maintains the organic relation of all
congregations in the church. It seeks to protect the church from
exploitation by ecclesiastical or secular power and ambition.
Every church order must be open to such reformation as may be
required to make it a more effective instrument of the mission
of reconciliation.

3. Revelation and Religion

The church in its mission encounters the religions of men and in
that encounter becomes conscious of its own human character as
a religion. God's revelation to Israel, expressed within Semitic
culture, gave rise to the religion of the Hebrew people. God's
revelation in Jesus Christ called forth the response of Jews and
Greeks and came to expression within Judaism and Hellenism as
the Christian religion. The Christian religion, as distinct from God's
revelation of himself, has been shaped throughout its history by
the cultural forms of its environment.

The Christian finds parallels between other religions and his
own and must approach all religions with openness and respect.
Repeatedly God has used the insight of non-Christians to challenge
the church to renewal. But the reconciling word of the gospel is
God's judgment upon all forms of religion, including the Christian.
The gift of God in Christ is for all men. The church, therefore, is
commissioned to carry the gospel to all men whatever their religion may be and even when they profess none.

4. Reconciliation in Society

In each time and place there are particular problems and crises through which God calls the church to act. The church, guided by the Spirit, humbled by its own complicity and instructed by all attainable knowledge, seeks to discern the will of God and learn how to obey in these concrete situations. The following are particularly urgent at the present time.

a. God has created the people of the earth to be one universal family. In his reconciling love he overcomes the barriers between brothers and breaks down every form of discrimination based on racial or ethnic difference, real or imaginary. The church is called to bring all men to receive and uphold one another as persons in all relationships of life: in employment, housing, education, leisure, marriage, family, church, and the exercise of political rights. Therefore the church labors for the abolition of all racial discrimination and ministers to those injured by it. Congregations, individuals, or groups of Christians who exclude, dominate, or patronize their fellowmen, however subtly, resist the Spirit of God and bring contempt on the faith which they profess.

b. God's reconciliation in Jesus Christ is the ground of the peace, justice, and freedom among nations which all powers of government are called to serve and defend. The church, in its own life, is called to practice the forgiveness of enemies and to commend to the nations as practical politics the search for cooperation and peace. This requires the pursuit of fresh and responsible relations across every line of conflict, even at risk to national security, to reduce areas of strife and to broaden international understanding. Reconciliation among nations becomes peculiarly urgent as countries develop nuclear, chemical, and biological weapons, diverting their manpower and resources from constructive uses and risking the annihilation of mankind. Although nations may serve God's purposes in history, the church which identifies the sovereignty of any one nation or any one way of life with the cause of God denies the Lordship of Christ and betrays its calling.

c. The reconciliation of man through Jesus Christ makes it plain that enslaving poverty in a world of abundance is an intolerable violation of God's good creation. Because Jesus identified himself with the needy and exploited, the cause of the world's poor is the cause of his disciples. The church cannot condone poverty, whether it is the product of unjust social structures, exploitation of the defenseless, lack of national resources, absence of technological understanding, or rapid expansion of populations. The church calls every man to use his abilities, his possessions, and the fruits of technology as gifts entrusted to him by God for the maintenance of his family and the advancement of the common welfare. It encourages those forces in human society that raise men's hopes for better conditions and provide them with opportunity for a decent living. A church that is indifferent to poverty, or evades responsibility in economic affairs, or is open to one social class only, or expects gratitude for its beneficence makes a mockery of reconciliation and offers no acceptable worship to God.

d. The relationship between men and women exemplifies in a basic way God's ordering of the interpersonal life for which he created mankind. Anarchy in sexual relationships is a symptom of man's alienation from God, his neighbor, and himself. Man's perennial confusion about the meaning of sex has been aggravated in our day by the availability of new means for birth control and the treatment of infection, by the pressures of urbanization, by the exploitation of sexual symbols in mass communication, and by world overpopulation. The church, as the household of God, is called to lead men out of this alienation into the responsible freedom of the new life in Christ. Reconciled to God, each person has joy in and respect for his own humanity and that of other persons; a man and woman are enabled to marry, to commit themselves to a mutually shared life, and to respond to each other in sensitive and lifelong concern; parents receive the grace to care for children in love and to nurture their individuality. The church comes under the judgment of God and invites rejection by man when it fails to lead men and women into the full meaning of life together, or withholds the compassion of Christ from those caught in the moral confusion of our time.

SECTION B. THE EQUIPMENT OF THE CHURCH

Jesus Christ has given the church preaching and teaching, praise and prayer, and Baptism and the Lord's Supper as means of fulfilling its service of God among men. These gifts remain, but the church is obliged to change the forms of its service in ways appropriate to different generations and cultures.

1. Preaching and Teaching

God instructs his church and equips it for mission through preaching and teaching. By these, when they are carried on in fidelity to the Scriptures and dependence upon the Holy Spirit, the people hear the word of God and accept and follow Christ. The message is addressed to men in particular situations. Therefore effective preaching, teaching, and personal witness require disciplined study of both the Bible and the contemporary world. All acts of public worship should be conducive to men's hearing of the gospel in a particular time and place and responding with fitting obedience.

2. Praise and Prayer

The church responds to the message of reconciliation in praise and prayer. In that response it commits itself afresh to its mission, experiences a deepening of faith and obedience, and bears open testimony to the gospel. Adoration of God is acknowledgement of the Creator by the creation. Confession of sin is admission of all men's guilt before God and of their need for his forgiveness. Thanksgiving is rejoicing in God's goodness to all men and in giving for the needs of others. Petitions and intercessions are addressed to God for the continuation of his goodness, the healing of men's ills, and their deliverance from every form of oppression. The arts, especially music and architecture, contribute to the praise and prayer of a Christian congregation when they help men to look beyond themselves to God and to the world which is the object of his love.

3. Baptism

By humble submission to John's baptism Christ joined himself to men in their need and entered upon his ministry of reconciliation in the power of the Spirit. Christian baptism marks the receiving of the same Spirit by all his people. Baptism with water represents not only cleansing from sin but a dying with Christ and a joyful rising with him to new life. It commits all Christians to die each day to sin and to live for righteousness. In baptism the church celebrates the renewal of the covenant with which God has bound his people to himself. By baptism individuals are publicly received into the church to share in its life and ministry, and the church becomes responsible for their training and support in Christian discipleship. When those baptized are infants the congregation, as well as the parents, has a special obligation to nurture them in the Christian life, leading them to make, by a public profession, a personal response to the love of God shown forth in their baptism.

4. The Lord's Supper

The Lord's Supper is a celebration of the reconciliation of men with God and with one another, in which they joyfully eat and drink together at the table of their Savior. Jesus Christ gave his church this remembrance of his dying for sinful men so that by participation in it they have communion with him and with all who shall be gathered to him. Partaking in him as they eat the bread and drink the wine in accordance with Christ's appointment, they receive from the risen and living Lord the benefits of his death and resurrection. They rejoice in the foretaste of the kingdom which he will bring to consummation at his promised coming, and go out from the Lord's Table with courage and hope for the service to which he has called them.

PART III: THE FULFILLMENT OF RECONCILIATION

God's redeeming work in Jesus Christ embraces the whole of man's life: social and cultural, economic and political, scientific and technological, individual and corporate. It includes man's natural environment as exploited and despoiled by sin. It is the will of God that his purpose for human life shall be fulfilled under the rule of Christ and all evil be banished from his creation.

Biblical visions and images of the rule of Christ such as a heavenly city, a father's house, a new heaven and earth, a marriage feast, and an unending day culminate in the image of the kingdom. The kingdom represents the triumph of God over all that resists his will and disrupts his creation. Already God's reign is present as a ferment in the world, stirring hope in men and preparing the world to receive its ultimate judgment and redemption.

With an urgency born of this hope the church applies itself to present tasks and strives for a better world. It does not identify limited progress with the kingdom of God on earth, nor does it despair in the face of disappointment and defeat. In steadfast hope the church looks beyond all partial achievement to the final triumph of God.

"Now to him who by the power at work within us is able to do far more abundantly than all we ask or think, to him be glory in the church and in Christ Jesus to all generations, forever and ever. Amen."

8. *Discussion Between Roman Catholics and Anglicans*

Christian Initiation

Report of a theological conference between representatives of the Anglican and Roman Catholic dioceses of Southwark, England.

The Third Theological Conference between representatives of the Church of England and the Roman Catholic Church in their respective dioceses of Southwark met at Digby Stuart College from Tuesday, 18th July to Friday, 21st July 1967. During the course of their deliberations they were honoured by visits from the Archbishop of the Roman Catholic diocese, the Most Reverend Cyril Cowderoy, and Dr. Mervyn Stockwood, Anglican Bishop of Southwark, and also from His Excellency the Most Reverend H. Cardinale, the Apostolic Delegate. At the close of their meeting the following statement, which is the private opinion of those involved and has no official status, was issued:

1. We have been concerned to study together the theology of Christian Initiation, together with its liturgical practice and pastoral implications.

2. We desire to record with a deep sense of gratitude that we find no significant differences amongst us greater than we should expect to find between different members within our

respective Communions, and certainly no differences either in theology or practice which would separate us as churches on this vitally important question.

3. We believe that despite the fact that we have been living apart from one another for some centuries, and although human frailty has often aggravated this tragic separation, the Holy Spirit has been at work among us, leading us closer to the fulness of truth, in such a way that we now find important areas of agreement in doctrine where there once existed apparently irreducible disagreements.

4. Every sacrament is a meeting between God and man. It takes place in the Church where Christ lives on as the point of encounter between man and God. God has first loved us in the sending of his Son into the world, and this is the ground of our sacramental life. Sacraments are gestures of God through Christ in the Church, inviting men to enter into a loving union with him.

5. At the same time, sacraments are the means by which men respond to this approach to God by living faith, without which a sacrament fails to be fruitful, not because God fails to offer himself, but because man fails to respond.

6. Nevertheless, when it involves the reception of a man into the Christian community, even though faith may be lacking or inadequate at the time of reception, it remains open to fulfilment at a later time, and as such cannot be repeated.

7. In general it is felt that misunderstanding of the nature of sacraments may often be avoided if they are described in such language of human relationship rather than in quasi-physical terms.

8. We desire to emphasize the unity of the baptism into which we were all baptized and on which so much ecumenical advance has been built, and in the light of the agreement in both theology and practice which we here record, we warmly welcome the instruction in the recent Roman Ecumenical Directory, para-

graphs 14-16 regarding the administration of conditional baptism only where there is real doubt about baptism already conferred.

9. We find, moreover, that we share a common unease and concern about our practice and consequent theological understanding of the rite of confirmation.

10. We would ask for a more serious consideration to be given to a reintegration of confirmation with the baptismal rite, apart from which we believe it cannot properly be understood.

11. This would mean a delegation of the power of confirmation to the parish priest, in order that children may receive communion at an early age if this is considered pastorally desirable, and would involve for Anglicans a consideration of the restoration of chrismation in order to safeguard the bishop's role in the initiatory rite, and for Roman Catholics the restoration of the traditional order of Baptism, Confirmation, First Communion.

12. A majority of us in both communions feel that it would then be desirable to consider the institution of a new rite of episcopal commissioning for mission and ministry on the threshold of adult life, for which the present rite of Confirmation is not suited, and the use of which for this purpose makes for theological confusion at an important point in the common experience of young Christians.

13. In strongly urging the consideration of such a rite, which would include a profession of faith and commitment, we recognise that this involves a much wider consideration of the nature of ministry for the lay members of the Church.

14. In commending this statement to the churches we serve, we give thanks to the Holy Spirit for the unity of mind and intention which has been vouchsafed us.

The Ministry of the Church

The agreements which follow have been reached by the under-signed members of the theological commission of the bilateral consultation appointed by the Catholic Bishops' Committee for Ecumenical and Interreligious Affairs and the North American Area Council of the World Alliance of Reformed Churches, and represent their present assessment of the question of the ministry of the Church.

1. SUMMARY OF DISCUSSIONS SO FAR HELD

For varying periods of time members of our commission have discussed ways and means by which our ministries could be united and each of us led to a deeper knowledge and love of the other. Our concern in the early meetings was to see how the road lay to full intercommunion. But it soon became clear that this end lay far beyond us, because the traditions of which we are a part have been separated for centuries and because there was not full acceptance amongst us of each other's ministries. At this point, therefore, in our discussion we moved away from churchly questions and asked, instead, particular and practical questions about the Church's ministry to the world. But this in turn forced us to inquire why in fact we remain separated from one another when the world's needs are so great, and to see if there may be a way of reconciliation. One inescapable fact of our present situation is the division of the church, a division which is a symbol of but also a scandal in an alienated and divided world. We know that we are charged with the responsibility of bringing healing to the broken human family, but we also know that in its own life the Church has contradicted and frustrated its purpose.

In the later meetings of the group, therefore, we turned to the needs of the world, hurt as it is by war, hungry and torn by riots, for it is this world and no other that provides us with the reason for our ministry and suggests to us new forms in which to express that ministry. Manifold opportunities for bearing effective Christian witness and service in the human family not only offer extraordinary possibilities for cooperative Christian living and ministry, but in our day are critical and urgent. Amongst these we think at once of cooperation in dealing with the urban crisis, the issues of war and peace, racial unrest, family life, and all matters involving human dignity. We think also, for example, of collaboration in the joint continuing education of all those who serve the church.

2. NORMS BY WHICH OUR MINISTRY IS SHAPED

Any form of ministry by the church is a participation in Christ's own ministry and servanthood. Those who would serve men must serve as their Master served. They must love and serve the actual world in which they live. But their ministry to this world is not a lordship, but a bond-service. It is not imposed as a rigid pattern, but undertaken willingly in new ways which express and fulfill the command of our Lord to go and teach and celebrate his sacraments.

Hence, the most decisive norm for contemporary forms of Christian ministry should be whether or not they enable men to understand, articulate and begin to realize their deepest needs—worship, love, justice, reconciliation and community, to name some of the most important. Any structures which effectively hinder the achievement of these needs or do not witness to the primary ministry of Christ must yield to other forms of ministry which do. In this context we acknowledge as an undiscussed problem the consequences or analogies which are to be drawn from the Lordship of Christ.

3. THE COMMON PRIESTHOOD

Within the Christian community all the faithful are called and empowered by the Holy Spirit to enter into and express the ministry of Christ. There is a whole range of gifts of the Spirit—gifts of service and love, rich in their diversity, not limited to the few, but possessed by men and women, young and old alike. All baptized and believing Christians share in the grace of God's Spirit, the freedom of the gospel, and the basic equality of the priestly people of God. It is our conviction that this doctrine of the common priesthood of the faithful needs to be magnified and lived out more within both our traditions. The Holy Spirit works where he wills and as he wills through all the people of God, calling them to their ministry. All Christians alike participate in the ministry of Christ to the world, serving, nourishing, healing and building up.

4. SPECIAL MINISTRIES

Within this community, where there is such diversity of gifts, some are also called by the Holy Spirit and ordained by the Church to undertake special ministries on behalf of the servants of Christ and through them on behalf of the world. This calling of some to nourish, heal and build up the household of faith in the ministry of word and sacraments is a particular gift of the Holy Spirit. Ordination to this ministry is therefore also a gift of the Spirit—it is a commissioning of persons by the Church and an invocation of the Spirit to empower them for their ministry. This empowering comes both from the Spirit and from the Church; the power given, however, is not power to dominate but to serve in Christ's stead and to do what he wills to be done for his world through his Church.

In this whole context we acknowledge as an undiscussed subject the ordination of women. In some Reformed Churches women are already ordained to the ministry of word and sacrament.

5. ORDINATION AND THE INDELIBLE CHARACTER

The Christian community prays at each ordination with the laying on of hands for the gift of the Spirit. To assert or to deny an ontic change at ordination can lead to a misunderstanding of its effect. Yet the new purpose toward which this person's life is directed through this commission to the ministry does truly and radically change the individual concerned, in the sense that he now bears and is implicated in a nexus of new relationships in the church and receives and exercises a new responsibility within its life.

There is a particular commission and charism in ordination to the special ministry of word and sacraments. The conceptions of ministerial order held by our respective traditions appear to be significantly different. In the Catholic tradition the priest in a particular way represents Christ to the people, but he himself is also a representative of the people before Christ. In the Reformed tradition ministerial order is not generally conceived of apart from pastoral functioning. When Roman Catholics speak of an indelible character conferred in ordination, their meaning is that the person who has been commissioned by the Church for this ministry retains during his life radical empowering to serve as priest, even though he ceases to exercise his priesthood. His ordination cannot be repeated any more than can his baptism. Reformed churchmen, while unwilling to speak of a conferring of an indelible character, do not deny the necessity of ordination in principle as long as the church continues on its pilgrimage, nor is reordination practiced among them. Both alike agree that the ordination is a gift by which the pilgrim church is enabled to serve the world until the kingdom of God is fully present.

6. VARIED HISTORICAL FORMS OF RULE IN THE CHURCH

In all ministries of the pilgrim church there are some permanent elements. There are also, however, some historically conditioned elements—naturally enough, since every ministry is a ministry incarnate at a particular place and time. The intense historical consciousness and research of our time and the study of the origins of our ministries show us clearly that many elements in them are historically conditioned. Thus, it is useful for Catholics to know that what is usually called the monarchical episcopate (found, for example, in St. Ignatius of Antioch in the second century) can be seen to be preceded by earlier and different forms, for instance, a collegial episcopate or government of presbyters, and so on. Presbyterian polity, on the other hand, though it is in intention an attempt to recover an early scheme of ministry, has also been historically conditioned. Recent historical studies indicate that there was a great variety of forms of ministry in the early church, and it seems clear that later patterns of ministry and priesthood were preceded by highly flexible and charismatic ministries. Modern patterns of ministry and priesthood can themselves be both flexible and charismatic, and we do not think that it is our task to reconstitute ancient forms in our day, though restoration of the married diaconate within the Roman Catholic church illustrates how earlier forms of ministry can be creatively reinterpreted in our day. But we can learn enough from the past to know that neither the monarchical episcopate nor any corporate polity have been the only legitimate forms of rule within the church.

7. THE IDEA OF THE PILGRIM CHURCH

Certain older ideas that equated the church with the Kingdom of God have to be corrected by modern theological and exegetical studies which have recovered for us an eschatological dimension in our thinking about church and ministry. Our whole thinking about the church has now a less absolute character than it had. The church's ministry at the present must be open to all the diverse ways by which the pilgrim church seeks to achieve its goal. This means that we must be ready for change and not confuse permanent elements in the ministry with passing ones. The paradigm of the Kingdom of God is of use to us here because it serves to draw us on in the hope that God's purposes will be fulfilled and indeed are beginning to be fulfilled through our existing ministries. But it also reminds us that we go, seeking a city. The Church is on the way, but it has not arrived. Our future hope and present limitation do something more for us: they help to shape our present ministries, adapting them for the future.

8. INTERCOMMUNION

No renunciation of the episcopate by the Roman Catholics is here proposed nor of their ministries by the representatives of the Reformed churches. What we do offer is a genuine statement of intention to move together to the future God will give us in the hope that the knowledge and love which have grown amongst us may encourage the appropriate authorities to help us both to move together toward this future.

If such an intention is given by us and a firm commitment given to each other, both the demands we face and the hopes we have confront us directly with the problem and the need of inter-communion. We recognize that theological convictions and pastoral sensitivity on both sides prevent us from acting without due care. At the same time we feel pain when we realize that, though we are one in many ways, at this central point we remain divided. It may yet be possible for us or for others to penetrate the theo-logical principles governing intercommunion in the hope of laying open the significance of the eucharist as the divinely given sacra-ment of unity and the medicine of our divisions. We, therefore, hope that God will soon give us the time and opportunity to take into our hands this means which he has given for repentance, reconciliation and unity.

The question of ultimate reconciliation and mutual acceptance can no longer be evaded and we know for certain that we shall return to it. In a broken world this reconciliation would be a sign of hope. In a world which has been drawn closer than ever to-gether, but is faced with the possibility of deeper division caused by war or other human tragedy, such a daring step would point men, we believe, to Christ, the Hope of the World.

9. QUESTIONS STILL AT ISSUE

Many questions still need to be discussed by us, for instance, the primacy of the Bishop of Rome, sacerdotal priesthood, the apos-tolic succession. To exclude these questions from our report may make a common statement on the ministry seem artificial, and we do not seek to awaken expectations which may be disappointed by further clarification we face in future discussions on the crucial issue or orders. Yet it has been possible for us to indicate at least these preliminary agreements and disagreements. The heavy emphases made in this paper and the lengthy discussion of problems of the ordained ministry may well appear to be a distortion, but they may also point out the way which leads us to full communion and liberate us for our ministry to the world.

THE MOST REV. ERNEST L. UNTERKOEFLER
THE REV. EUGENE BURKE, CSP
THE REV. LUKE STEINER, OSB
THE REV. KILIAN MCDONNELL, OSB
THE REV. DANIEL O'HANLON, S.J.
DR. LEONARD SWIDLER
THE REV. ROBERT MCAFEE BROWN
THE REV. M. EUGENE OSTERHAVEN
THE REV. JOHN V. THOMAS, O.P.
THE REV. ANDREW HARSANYI
MRS. MARGRETHE B. J. BROWN
THE REV. JAMES H. NICHOLS
THE REV. ROSS MACKENZIE
THE REV. JOHN L. MCKENZIE, S.J.
THE REV. ROBERT C. MOSS, JR.